LIVING IN THE LIGHT OF INEXTINGUISHABLE HOPE

THE GOSPEL ACCORDING TO THE OLD TESTAMENT

*A series of studies on the lives
of Old Testament characters, written for
laypeople and pastors, and designed to
encourage Christ-centered reading, teaching,
and preaching of the Old Testament*

IAIN M. DUGUID
Series Editor

LIVING IN THE LIGHT OF INEXTINGUISHABLE HOPE

THE GOSPEL ACCORDING TO
JOSEPH

IAIN M. DUGUID AND
MATTHEW P. HARMON

P&R PUBLISHING

P.O. BOX 817 • PHILLIPSBURG • NEW JERSEY 08865-0817

Unless otherwise indicated, Scripture quotations are from *ESV Bible®* (*The Holy Bible, English Standard Version®*). Copyright © 2001 by Crossway Bibles, a publishing ministry of Good News Publishers. Used by permission. All rights reserved.

Scripture quotations marked (NIV) are from the HOLY BIBLE, NEW INTERNATIONAL VERSION®. NIV®. Copyright © 1973, 1978, 1984 by International Bible Society. Used by permission of Zondervan Publishing House. All rights reserved.

Italics within Scripture quotations indicate emphasis added.

ISBN: 978-1-59638-542-9 (pbk)
ISBN: 978-1-59638-709-6 (ePub)
ISBN: 978-1-59638-710-2 (Mobi)

Printed in the United States of America

Library of Congress Cataloging-in-Publication Data

Duguid, Iain M.
   Living in the light of inextinguishable hope : the Gospel according to Joseph / Iain M. Duguid and Matthew P. Harmon.
      pages cm. -- (The Gospel according to the Old Testament)
   Includes bibliographical references and index.
   ISBN 978-1-59638-542-9 (pbk.)
   1. Joseph (Son of Jacob) 2. Bible. O.T. Genesis XXXVII-L--Criticism, interpretation, etc. 3. Typology (Theology) I. Title.
   BS580.J6D84 2013
   222'.1106--dc23
                                                          2012050206

To Barb and Rebecca

CONTENTS

FOREWORD

The New Testament is in the Old concealed;
the Old Testament is in the New revealed.
—Augustine

C oncerning this salvation, the prophets who prophesied about the grace that was to be yours searched and inquired carefully, inquiring what person or time the Spirit of Christ in them was indicating when he predicted the sufferings of Christ and the subsequent glories. It was revealed to them that they were serving not themselves but you, in the things that have now been announced to you through those who preached the good news to you by the Holy Spirit sent from heaven, things into which angels long to look. (1 Peter 1:10–12)

"Moreover, some women of our company amazed us. They were at the tomb early in the morning, and when they did not find his body, they came back saying that they had even seen a vision of angels, who said that he was alive. Some of those who were with us went to the tomb and found it just as the women had said, but him they did not see." And he said to them, "O foolish ones, and slow of heart to believe all that the prophets have spoken! Was it not necessary that the Christ should suffer these things and enter into his glory?" And beginning with Moses and all the Prophets, he interpreted to them in all the Scriptures the things concerning himself. (Luke 24:22–27)

The prophets searched. Angels longed to see. And the disciples didn't understand. But Moses, the Prophets, and all the Old Testament Scriptures had spoken about it—that Jesus would come, suffer, and then be glorified. God began to tell a story in the Old Testament, the ending of which the audience eagerly anticipated. But the Old Testament audience was left hanging. The plot was laid out, but the climax was delayed. The unfinished story begged for an ending. In Christ, God has provided the climax to the Old Testament story. Jesus did not arrive unannounced; his coming was declared *in advance* in the Old Testament—not just in explicit prophecies of the Messiah, but also by means of the stories of all the events, characters, and circumstances in the Old Testament. God was telling a larger, overarching, unified story. From the account of creation in Genesis to the final stories of the return from exile, God progressively unfolded his plan of salvation. And the Old Testament account of that plan always pointed in some way to Christ.

AIMS OF THIS SERIES

The Gospel According to the Old Testament series was begun by my former professors, Tremper Longman and Al Groves, to whom I owe an enormous personal debt of gratitude. I learned from them a great deal about how to recognize the gospel in the Old Testament. I share their deep conviction that the Bible, both Old and New Testaments, is a unified revelation of God and that its thematic unity is found in Christ. This series of studies will continue to pursue their initial aims:

- to lay out the pervasiveness of the revelation of Christ in the Old Testament

- to promote a Christ-centered reading of the Old Testament
- to encourage Christ-centered preaching and teaching from the Old Testament

These volumes are written primarily for pastors and lay-people, not scholars. They are designed in the first instance to serve the church, not the academy.

My hope and prayer remain the same as Tremper and Al's: that this series will continue to encourage the revival of interest in the Old Testament as a book that constantly points forward to Jesus Christ, to his sufferings and the glories that would follow.

IAIN M. DUGUID

ACKNOWLEDGMENTS

Many people work very hard to enable a book to see the light of day. We would like to begin by thanking all of the people at P&R Publishing, especially Marvin Padgett and Aaron Gottier, for their encouragement, professionalism, and commitment to excellence in overseeing the production of this book.

I (Iain) acknowledge my debt of gratitude to my wife, Barb. Thank you for all you have taught me about sin (mostly mine), grace, repentance, and love for the gospel. By reading each sermon and commenting along the way, you have contributed greatly to the applicability and usefulness of these messages and prevented me from uttering many of the insensitive and thoughtless ideas to which I am prone. Thank you as well to my children (Wayne, Jamie, Sam, Hannah, Rob, and Rosie). As you start to leave home and head off to populate other churches, the front row seems increasingly empty without you. I'm so glad that each of you has had a chance to be part of the Grove City adventure with us.

I would also like to thank the enthusiastic congregation of Christ Presbyterian Church. It is always a delight to open up God's Word to you, knowing that you are eager and hungry for the gospel. What more could any pastor wish for? Well, help in the ministry, for one thing. So thank you from the bottom of my heart to Matt for answering God's call to come to Grove City and bring organization, vision, maturity, and a servant's heart to our church plant. As an answer to our fervent prayers, you and Rebecca are truly more than we could have imagined.

I (Matt) would like to thank my beautiful wife, Rebecca. Thank you for your constant love and companionship, your patience with my sin, and your encouragement in all my endeavors. *C'est à cause de toi.* . . . To my children, Anastasia and Ransom, thank you for your smiles, laughs, hugs, and excitement about exploring God's world. Every day you remind me that we all—even, and especially, Papa—need to say sorry and that Jesus loves us very much.

While indebted to many others, I also wish to express profound appreciation to our two most recent church families. To Hope Presbyterian Church, thank you for embracing our family during our graduate school sojourning and for giving me an opportunity to serve you, first as an intern and then as assistant pastor. Special thanks go to David Rowe and the session for invaluable ministry experience, as well as their joyful readiness to prepare us for whatever future ministry God provided.

Likewise, my deep thanks go to Christ Presbyterian Church for your warm reception of us to Grove City. Your deep love of God and his gospel is a constant delight. We never imagined that we would feel at home with a new church family in such a short time. I especially want to thank Iain and Barb for their enthusiastic welcome and invitation to labor together in proclaiming the reconciling work of God in the life, death, and resurrection of our Lord Jesus.

Iain Duguid
Matt Harmon

CHAPTER ONE

HOPE FOR DYSFUNCTIONAL FAMILIES (GENESIS 37:1–11)

Some towns and cities seem to be misnamed. My wife grew up in Mount Morris, Michigan—elevation: a whopping 774 feet. People wore T-shirts proudly proclaiming: "I climbed Mount Morris." It is probably not the only misnamed place in America. Take Philadelphia, for example. It is a great city, famous as the home of the Liberty Bell and Independence Hall, whose very name means "brotherly love." Yet some of their sports fans don't seem to have got the message. Where else would Santa Claus get booed and pelted with snowballs, as he once was at an Eagles football game? Not much brotherly love there, it seems.

A COMMUNITY OF NATIONS

Genesis 37 is not about brotherly love, either, but rather about brotherly hate. The theme word "brother" occurs no less than twenty-one times in this chapter, yet this is a story about brothers who cannot get along. Actually, brothers don't get along well anywhere in Genesis. The theme of brother against brother started with Cain and Abel and continued down through the generations with

1

Isaac and Ishmael, followed by Jacob and Esau. Clearly, God did not choose Abraham's family because they were a better representative of traditional family values than their pagan neighbors—unless you count favoritism and murderous envy as the traditional values of this family.

The same pattern continues as we enter the story of the next generation in Genesis 37. In the introduction to a story, you expect to encounter the main characters and plot conflicts that will make up the body of the story. This introduction is no exception: here we meet the main characters—Joseph, his brothers, and their father Jacob—and the main complication of the plot, which is the fact that Joseph's brothers hate him.

Notice how that hostility immediately recalibrates the way that we think about this story, which we tend to assume is about Joseph and his coat of many colors. Of course, Joseph is central to what follows in many ways, even if his special coat is a rather incidental detail. Yet this is not simply Joseph's story, nor is God at work only in and through Joseph. This is actually a story about Joseph *and his brothers*, which makes perfect sense if you think about the original audience for whom Moses was writing in the wilderness. Joseph and his brothers were the founding fathers of the nation of Israel, a group of flawed and deeply sinful individuals whom God chose to make into a nation belonging to him. In fact, the story of Genesis 37–50 is not even just about Joseph and his brothers; it is a key part of the story about God's grand plan for Israel and what he is up to in the lives of his people as a whole.

Earlier in the book of Genesis, the Lord affirmed that from Jacob would come a community of nations (Gen. 35:11; cf. 28:3). Significantly, the Hebrew word used here is *qahal*, which literally means "congregation" or even "church," since the Greek translation of the Old Testament most often renders it by *ekklesia*.[1] In contrast to the previous generations, when God sovereignly chose one member of the family to bear the line of promise instead of the other (electing Isaac over Ishmael, and Jacob over Esau), this time God promised that he would choose all twelve of Jacob's sons and make them into a harmonious, worshipping community, the nation of Israel. Indeed, the initial readers of the story, the Israelites in the time of Moses, were a fulfillment of that promise. Moses wanted them to look back and remember that there were times when that promise of creating a harmoniously united, worshipping people looked every bit as impossible for God to fulfill as his earlier promise to give a child to an elderly and barren couple. Yet against all odds and against all of the evil schemes of sinful men, including those whom he had chosen, God would nonetheless achieve his goal of a united, worshipping community.

God's ultimate purpose was not just to create and choose the Israel of Moses' day to be his worshipping community, however. Rather, his goal was to create for himself a renewed and restored Israel, the spiritual descendants of Abraham, who would together form a united, worshipping family in Christ that would go beyond the physical descendants of Israel and encompass people from every nation and tribe on earth.

JOSEPH

First, though, we'll explore what God was up to with this particular dysfunctional family, starting with the least obviously messed-up member, Joseph. We might easily assume that because Joseph is the hero of the story, he must be perfect in everything that he does. Not so. The first appearance of a biblical character on the stage of a narrative is always important, and Joseph is no exception. We meet him at seventeen years of age, sent out into the fields to help his brothers with the sheep. The text says, "He was a boy with the sons of Bilhah and Zilpah" (Gen. 37:2), but this is actually as much a job description as it is a reference to his age. He was sent along with his brothers to do all of the menial and unimportant jobs. Other biblical characters also spent time as shepherds, of course, notably Moses and David. But instead of receiving revelations from God while he was a shepherd, like Moses, or protecting his sheep from the lion and the bear, like David, what did Joseph do? He brought home a "bad report" of his brothers to his father (37:2).

In English, a "bad report" can be either true or false. In Hebrew, however, this particular phrase has the connotations of a false or malicious report.[2] The spies brought the same kind of "bad report" back to the people of Israel from the land of Canaan, telling them that it was not worth fighting for (Num. 13:32). In Proverbs 10:18, the word is translated "slander." Joseph did not like his brothers, or perhaps he did not like being a servant to his brothers, and so he brought back a fabricated or exaggerated account to their father of their misdeeds. He played his own part in perpetuating the divisions in the household between the children of different mothers, a conflict highlighted by calling them "the sons of Bilhah and Zilpah" (37:2; cf. 29:31–30:24).

In addition, there is Joseph's handling of his dreams. First, he saw himself harvesting the grain with his brothers, when suddenly their eleven sheaves of grain bowed down to his sheaf (Gen. 37:7). After that, he had another dream, in which the sun, the moon, and eleven stars bowed down to him (37:9). Joseph already knew that his brothers hated him for his favored position. Yet when he recounted the dreams that declared that he was not only their father's favorite, but apparently God's chosen favorite as well, he seems to have been rubbing their noses in his exaltation. It is one thing, perhaps, for Joseph to tell them the first dream. Yet in the face of their bitter response to that dream, for Joseph then to turn around and recount to them the second dream suggests insensitivity on a massive scale.

I'm sure you've met people like that in your own experience—people who are in danger of being spoiled by too much success too young. It might be a freshman who becomes the starting quarterback of the football team or has the lead in the play, a young professional who rapidly makes a killing on Wall Street, or even a young preacher whose first church grows and blossoms rapidly. As a result of that quick success, they become full of themselves. They may have a great deal of talent, but that talent is in danger of going to waste or of corrupting them, unless something profound happens to turn them around. Joseph desperately needed help.

JACOB

Then there is Jacob's dysfunction as the father of the family. The special coat was not the first indicator of Jacob's preference for Joseph. When Jacob returned to the Promised Land after his sojourn in Paddan-aram and had to face Esau, he heard that Esau was coming to meet him with four hundred men, and he was terrified that Esau was planning a massacre. For that reason, young Joseph and his mother Rachel were safely tucked away at the back of the caravan, while his older brothers and their mothers were left exposed at the front (Gen. 33:2). How do you think it made the brothers feel to know that their father regarded them as expendable?

That brings us to Joseph's richly ornamented coat (Gen. 37:3). It was not necessarily a coat of many colors, as tradition has it, following the Greek translation; however, in the only other place where this phrase occurs in the Bible, it refers to a royal garment (2 Sam. 13:18). Whatever precise kind of robe it was, it was certainly not the kind of clothing you would wear if you were planning to work. That makes it striking that we hear about this robe *after* Joseph has brought the bad report to his father about his brothers.

There is a definite sequence here: Joseph goes to serve and work under his brothers while they are shepherding; he brings home a bad report about them; his father rewards him with a splendid coat. The next time the brothers go out shepherding, later in the chapter, Joseph is no longer working with them. Presumably, he's back home in his fancy coat, with his feet up on the couch, while his brothers are out in the fields. No wonder his brothers hated him!

Of course, Jacob was repeating the toxic family pattern from his own youth. It is tragically true that we often perpetuate the family dysfunction that we saw around us as children. In Jacob's childhood family, his father Isaac preferred Esau, while Jacob was his mother's favorite; now he turned around and did the same thing to his own children. How tragic to pass that dysfunction on to the next generation! Yet there was probably also a spiritual dimension to Jacob's preference for Joseph. In verse 3, the narrator tells us that Jacob loved Joseph because he was "the son of his old age." We might rather have expected to hear that Jacob loved Joseph because he was the son of his favorite wife, Rachel, which is certainly also true. But calling Joseph "the son of his old age" links him with Isaac, the child that Sarah bore to Abraham in his old age: the same word is used of Isaac in Genesis 21:2. This suggests that Jacob loved Joseph more than his brothers because he believed that he would be the child that God had promised, the one who would carry on the promised line of the Messiah, the promised seed of the woman of Genesis 3:15.

That expectation was probably deepened and furthered by Joseph's dreams that his siblings and parents would come and bow down to him. Surely here was confirmation from God that Joseph was indeed the chosen one. The image of a father and mother bowing before their own child is outrageous in a patriarchal society, so Jacob rebuked Joseph, yet at the same time he "kept the saying in mind" (Gen. 37:11). This is the same response that Mary had to Jesus' childhood adventure with the teachers in the temple in Jerusalem (Luke 2:51). Both parents wondered and pondered what these things might mean about their special child.

THE BROTHERS

There was no wondering and pondering on the part of Joseph's brothers. They were united in hating the dreamer. They already hated him so much after he received his coat that they couldn't even greet him: literally, the text says, "They couldn't say '*Shalom*' to him" (Gen. 37:4). That was before the dreams started. After the dreams, they hated him all the more (37:8). Don't forget that these were danger-ous men, too. Reuben had already shown his disregard for both morality and the family structure by sleeping with his father's concubine, Bilhah, an act that had more to do with rebellion than with lust (35:22). Simeon and Levi had massacred an unsuspecting town back in chapter 34, while Jacob did nothing to stop them. There is an ominous atmosphere in this story, even before we get to the events later in the chapter. This is a family desperately in need of divine intervention.

BUT GOD . . .

But don't forget about God. Even though the Lord's name is not mentioned in the passage, that doesn't mean that he is not active. Throughout the Joseph narrative, God is visible primarily through his acts of providence, working all of the details of the story together to bring about his own purposes in the lives of each of the characters. Here in this passage, God's most obvious action is sending Joseph the dreams. What was God thinking? Why did he toss a lighted match into such a powder keg of family dysfunction, well knowing the pain, heartache, and suffering that would inevitably result? You don't have to be an omniscient deity to see where this story is likely to end up!

Yet it is precisely because he is an omniscient and sovereign deity that God can do this. He knew exactly how Joseph would respond to the dreams, as well as exactly how Jacob and the brothers would respond. None of the circumstances of their lives were outside God's sovereign control for a microsecond. He knew what would happen and how he would use every scrap of the pain, suffering, and dysfunction to shape the individual lives of the members of this family into something noble and great, and thus to accomplish his own redemptive purposes, both for this family and, through them, for the entire world. There was nothing careless about God sending Joseph the dreams: it was all part of his perfect plan to bring into being his chosen, united, worshipping community.

Yet it is worth noting that God's redemptive ways are not ours. Which of us would choose to grow up in a dysfunctional family that would explode in violent and traumatic sin? Which of us would choose to be sold as a slave and carried into an alien culture? The answer is clearly, "No one." Yet that was God's perfect plan for Joseph. In our own lives, we quickly assume that wherever terrible abuse takes place, or relationships tragically fall apart, or traumatic sin blights our lives, that God must surely be absent. Nothing could be further from the truth. Certainly, God hates sin and abuse. He neither causes sin nor condones it. We are responsible for our own sin, which flows from our own wicked hearts (James 1:13–14). Yet God's redemptive pathways do not lead us around conflict, abuse, divorce, and broken families, or even away from the expression and outworking of our own sinful natures. Instead, his perfect plan for our lives often takes us right through the eye of the storm, where our dysfunction and sin, along with that of our families and friends, is on full and tragic display, so that the gospel of his powerful grace and sovereign mercy can be equally powerfully on display.

GOD'S TRAINING PROGRAM OF SUFFERING

What was God up to in all of this? In the first place, there was a work he needed to do in Joseph's heart. Joseph was not yet ready to be a leader. He was a brash, overconfident, self-centered young man at this stage, and he needed to be prepared in God's classic school of church leadership, which involved a lengthy period of cooling his heels on the sidelines, waiting for what God had in store for him. Joseph would be prepared through trials, temptations, and suffering until God decided he was ready to step onto the stage in his service. The path of spiritual growth for Joseph involved abuse and mistreatment, separation from home and family, having his character dragged through the mud, and finally being neglected and forgotten for years by the very people he had helped. But this training process was necessary to make him into the person God was calling him to be. It was precisely these trials and difficulties that would show Joseph his weakness as well as his strength, and cast him back repeatedly on his need to rely on God. These were lessons that he could never learn while sitting at home comfortably in his father's house, dressed in his fancy coat.

Yet, at the same time, God also gave Joseph dreams at the outset of his difficult journey. The dreams were the trigger that launched his brothers' hatred into action, but they were also given to Joseph to build in him a solid hope in God's promise. Joseph would later have to return to those dreams time and time again, trusting that the God who gave them to him would in due time fulfill them, no matter how unlikely that might have seemed.

Perhaps you are in this phase of God's training program right now. You feel like your life is on hold—or worse, that God has completely forgotten about you. Maybe your gifts have not been recognized, or there is no opportunity for you to use them right now; perhaps you have been mis-understood and mistreated by the church community, and you wonder if God will ever open a door for you to serve in a meaningful way. Perhaps you are seeing your whole life explode around you right now in a catastrophic maelstrom of sin, whether your own or that of others. Perhaps you have personally experienced abuse from your own family or from authority figures around you, even from within the church.

How should you respond to this period of life? You don't have personal dreams like Joseph to fall back on, explaining God's plan for your life. But you have something better: you have the solid promises of God that, having begun a good work in you, he will bring it to completion (Phil. 1:6). It may be that this period of painful training will equip you to serve God more fully further down the road. In other cases, it may not be so easy to see the plan in what God is doing. Yet we know that he is always at work and that he will bring that work to completion on the day of Christ Jesus. During the dark days of trial and suffering, therefore, hold on to God's assurance that he will use your life in the way that he sees fit to bring glory to himself, and that that path will also be good for you. God's training route for you may take you along a path that you would never have chosen for yourself, a path that will wind through the valley of deep shadow and take you into battles from which you will emerge with wounds whose depth only you and he know. Yet he will nonetheless be with you every step of the way, as he has promised, shaping you for greatness in his sight through each of those difficult and painful experiences.

GOD'S TRAINING PROGRAM OF SIN

Joseph's brothers were not ready for leadership over God's people yet, either. Their training ground would be different from Joseph's, however. Joseph was prepared through the school of hard knocks and difficult providences, in which he would suffer a wide variety of abuse and mis-treatment. He would learn by being sinned against. His brothers, meanwhile, would suffer none of these things. Their schooling involved a double major in the departments of sin and repentance. They would learn about their own depravity by bitter experience. Would the brothers have imagined that they could stoop to the depths of contem-plating the murder of their own brother and then selling him as a slave? Certainly they hated him, but enough to do something like that? After they tossed Joseph into a pit, they were not immediately wracked with remorse; instead, they casually sat down to eat a meal together (Gen. 37:25) while their brother's life hung by a thread. Then they cal-lously deceived their father into thinking that his beloved son had been killed and eaten by a wild animal (37:31–33).

Out of all of the brothers, Judah would have a par-ticularly intense schooling in the training program of sin and repentance. Would Judah have thought that he could casually pursue a roadside prostitute and then hypocritically insist that if his daughter-in-law had been promiscuous, she must die (Gen. 38:24)? As we track Judah's story, we'll see him change and his heart soften precisely through the experience of his own sin and its exposure, to the point where he was finally ready to give up his own life, rather than see his brother Benjamin imprisoned and his father's heart broken a second time. The experience of his own sin and its aftermath transformed Judah and, through the work of God, made him into a different person.

Maybe this is where you find yourself right now: in the pit of seeing your own sinfulness clearly, perhaps for the first time. You may find it profoundly puzzling that God does not protect you more from sin. After all, you pray repeatedly, "Lead me not into temptation," yet temptation seems to come seeking you anyway, and you fall repeat-edly into the same patterns of disobedience. Perhaps these patterns of sin are secret, known only to yourself. Or per-haps they are public knowledge, so that everyone in your community knows what a great sinner you are. Possibly you sinned under great provocation after resisting for a long time. Or perhaps you gave in easily, in spite of all of the blessings and comforts that God had showered upon you. Either way, God is as completely sovereign over your sin as he is over your circumstances. You cannot even sin outside the will of God. So what is God doing when he turns you over to your own sin in this way? Why doesn't God reach down and stop you in time?

The answer is that our sin is also part of God's training program for us. As we said earlier, God is not the author of our sin; it comes readily enough from us. All he has to do is leave us to ourselves, and we will give in to temptation in whatever shape or form it comes. That is why there is so much sin around us and within our own hearts. Is the church today any better than the original Israel, the dysfunctional family of twelve brothers who couldn't get along? We each shame the name of Christ daily through our anger, our malicious words and actions, our pride, our gossip, our rumor spreading designed to bring others down and exalt ourselves. It happens in our families, our communities, and in our churches. By the grace and gift of God, I happen to be a hard-working person who can measure up to a certain standard of outward righteousness. Yet how quickly I confuse that gift of God with something I do myself, and imagine that the good things that I do come from within me. That attitude makes me a proud and judgmental person with little compassion for those who are weak and struggling. It is easy for me to mock and condemn others for their weaknesses and failures. It is a way of pumping myself up and trying to show God that I ought to be the favorite of his children because of how hard I work for him. In short, it is sin, a self-glorifying heart attitude that easily emerges in ungracious words toward others.

Yet God has good purposes even for my sin. God can use my inability to control my tongue to expose my arrogance and to humble me. In this way, I gain a greater appreciation of grace than I would have if God sovereignly enabled me to restrain my sinful heart. Our sin repeatedly chastens us and shows us that God did not choose us because of what wonderful people we are. Far from it, we are profoundly broken and rebellious people, who left to ourselves cannot remain faithful to him for an instant. But our God is a great savior for great sinners, like Joseph's brothers and like us, a God who revels in rescuing and redeeming hopeless cases and lost causes and turning them into a united community who together worship him and sing of his grace, not of their own goodness.

JACOB

Finally, God's work in Jacob was not complete yet. This may seem strange and discouraging to us, as Jacob was already well on his way to becoming an old man. He had been in God's training school of suffering for many years; his own sin had repeatedly been exposed, and he had been brought to repentance many times. Although he had learned many lessons in God's school, he had still made only small beginnings on the road to righteousness. One moment he was the old Jacob, full of self-centeredness, focused entirely on his own needs and desires, while the next he was the Israel of God, the man who clings to God and trusts him for blessing in spite of all his circumstances. Even after all these years of learning, he still had further to go, a few more rounds in the training ring where he would learn once again that God's providence can be trusted to fulfill what he has promised.

Maybe this is where you are today: puzzled by the slowness of your spiritual growth. You thought that you should have arrived at a greater degree of holiness by now. At this stage in your life, you should have a more stable trust in Christ and a greater measure of personal holiness.

What is God up to in your life? He is showing you that you will never outgrow your need of his grace and power. You will need his strength every bit as much when you are eighty-five as when you are five, fifteen, or forty-five. As long as you live in this world, you will experience the fact that you are both saint and sinner. You are as justified today as you ever will be by Christ's righteousness, and yet in some ways you may be as far from living out the full implications of that reality as you ever have been.

JESUS

We will all struggle with that reality until Christ returns. For this narrative is not merely about what God is up to in the lives of Jacob, Joseph, and his brothers. It is about what God is doing in redeeming a people for himself in Christ. In the same way, your story is part of that larger story of God's redeeming purpose. The dreams in this chapter are too big to be merely about Joseph. To be sure, they foreshadow later events, when Joseph's brothers will come down to Egypt and bow down to him. Yet when Jacob blesses his sons in Genesis 49, he tells Judah, not Joseph, that his father's sons will bow down before him. It is from the tribe of Judah that the one will come of whom the promise in Genesis 3 speaks. Joseph's life foreshadows Christ's life in profound ways, but he is not the Christ himself. The promised Christ will be the son of Judah's line, yet he will be far greater even than Judah: he is God himself, the one before whom the sun, the moon, and the stars themselves truly bow.

Yet this glorious Messiah, the God-man Jesus Christ, willingly humbled himself and entered the school of suffering and temptation. He set aside the deserved robe of honor and the safe place at his Father's side as the chosen favorite. The firstborn of all creation left behind his glory and the constant praise of angels and archangels, and exposed himself to a world that would reject him, scorn him, hate him, abuse him, and ultimately kill him. During his earthly ministry, his own brothers did not believe in him (John 7:5). How painful that must have been—yet he never responded with hatred in return. He never built himself up at the expense of others or mocked weak and broken sinners. He could justly have been filled with pride, impatient with foolish and sinful people, but instead he was humble and gentle, kind and compassionate to those weighed down by their own sin. We quickly judge and condemn anyone who doesn't measure up to our standards of righteousness, but Jesus was patient and long-suffering with sinners, even those who nailed him to the cross.

What was the Father thinking, willingly sending his beloved Son into such a powder keg of fallen and sinful humanity, giving him a physical body that could be tortured and wounded? He was thinking of you and me, of the church that he was creating and calling into existence—a new, united, worshipping community of redeemed sinners. To reach that goal, Jesus took upon himself the punishment that all of your sin deserves, so that now the discovery of your sin need not destroy you, but instead leads you to marvel afresh at the wonder of God's grace. To accomplish that purpose, Jesus endured the heavenly Father's rejection on the cross, where all of God's perfect and pure hatred of sin was poured out on his head. He was forsaken and abandoned by his own Father, placed under a curse, so that we might be included forever in the Father's blessing.

As a result, your standing before God does not depend upon your best efforts to love your brothers and sisters, whether in your literal family or in the church. Ask God to help you respond to his marvelous grace by showing a similar grace to those around you. However, never forget that though you are called to try hard, you will often fail in these things, putting others down and puffing yourself up. You will continue to sin against your siblings and friends, just as they will sin against you. Look afresh, therefore, to

Jesus' perfect obedience, and praise him that in Christ the gospel provides marvelous hope and rest for the most broken of individuals and the most dysfunctional of families.

FOR FURTHER REFLECTION

1. What kind of community did God promise to create through the family of Abraham?
2. How did each member of Joseph's family (Joseph, Jacob, and the brothers) undermine community and contribute to the dysfunction of the family?
3. How have you felt broken community in either your family or your church? What did you contribute to the dysfunction?
4. How did God act providentially in the circumstances that led to the brothers selling Joseph? Has God brought healing through upheaval in any of your relationships?
5. In what ways do you identify with Joseph's suffering, the brothers' sin, and Jacob's slow spiritual growth? What do these experiences reveal about your own heart?
6. How does the perfect life and sin-bearing suffering of Jesus overcome our disunity? In what specific ways could the good news of Jesus' brotherly embrace transform relationships in your immediate and church family?

CHAPTER TWO

SHATTERED DREAMS (GENESIS 37:12–36)

I n the musical *Les Misérables*, Fantine sings a song called "I Dreamed a Dream." As she reflects on how, in her younger days, she fell in love with a handsome young student who abandoned her, leaving her pregnant and alone, she sadly sings, "Now life has killed the dream I dreamed."[1] Her hopes and dreams had been crushed by events, leaving her floundering in the pit of despair, buffeted by a hurricane she knows she cannot withstand.

We would all like to believe that we couldn't possibly end up like Fantine, with the narrative of our lives so badly derailed. Yet the truth is that the vessels of our lives are fragile craft, easily overturned by the powerful storms of life, whether in the form of serious sickness, the death of a loved one, a broken marriage, an abusive relationship, a debilitating accident, or the failure to achieve your career hopes and ambitions. The storms of life can indeed be severe, and they are not easily weathered. Yet in Genesis 37 we see how even though it may have seemed that Joseph's God-given dreams were shattered in pieces, the Lord was still in complete control of every aspect of his life. In fact, the Lord was at work precisely in and through the shattering experience of suffering terrible abuse at the hands of his own brothers. This turned out to be the means by which the Lord accomplished his own good purposes for Joseph, for the entire family, and ultimately for the entire world.

THE PURSUIT OF SHALOM

First, let's look at what happened to Joseph. We have already seen what a dysfunctional family God chose as the foundation for the worshipping community that would become Israel. Joseph brought home a critical report about his brothers (Gen. 37:2), which Jacob rewarded with a royal robe (37:3), a symbol of his favoritism for Joseph over all of his brothers. Meanwhile, Joseph's brothers hated him, not just for the bad report and the royal robe, but also "for his dreams and for his words" (37:8). It reached the point where they hated Joseph so much that they couldn't even say *shalom* to him when they met him around the house (37:4).

Yet, in spite of this toxic home environment, Jacob sent Joseph off to Shechem, where his brothers had gone to pasture the sheep, to inquire after their welfare (their *shalom*, 37:14). What was Jacob thinking? How did he imagine that the brothers would greet Joseph miles away from home, especially when he arrived wearing his fancy coat? Yet Joseph went obediently at his father's command to look for his brothers. At first, his search was fruitless, and Joseph could easily have given up and gone home, explaining that he had tried to find his brothers but had failed. Yet at the crucial moment, while wandering in a field near Shechem, Joseph happened to meet a man who had the information he needed (37:15). This man not only took the trouble to ask Joseph what he was looking for, but was quite possibly the only man in the whole area who knew where Joseph's brothers had gone—to Dothan. If this man had taken a stroll in the opposite direction, the story would have turned out quite differently.

THE MASTER OF DREAMS

Armed with this information, Joseph went on to Dothan, where he found his brothers (Gen. 37:17). More precisely, they saw Joseph coming from a distance and plotted against him. "Here comes this master of dreams," they said. "Let's kill him and throw him into a pit, saying that a fierce animal killed him, and then we'll see what becomes of his dreams" (see 37:19–20). At this point, the oldest brother, Reuben, intervened. He suggested that, instead of shedding their brother's blood, they simply cast him into a dry pit. Apparently, his plan was to rescue Joseph and bring him back safely to their father, perhaps to get himself back into his father's favor (37:22). Heeding Reuben's advice, the brothers did not kill Joseph right away, but merely stripped off his robe and threw him into an empty pit (37:23–24). Then they sat down to eat their pita and hummus sandwiches, as if this were just another ordinary day.

As the brothers were eating their lunch, along came a caravan of merchants who were headed down to Egypt, and Judah had a still better idea. "Rather than spilling our brother's blood," he said, "let us sell him to these Ishmaelites. That way we won't be guilty of shedding our brother's blood, and we'll actually make some money in the transaction. After all, he is our brother—our own flesh and blood! He will still end up being dead to us, of course, but without any of the messiness" (see 37:26–27). So they sold Joseph to the traders for twenty shekels of silver, a typical price for a slave in the early second millennium (37:28). Legally, of course, the difference between selling into slavery and outright murder is a distinction without a difference. Selling someone into slavery was a capital offense in ancient Near Eastern law, just as murder was, because in either case you were stealing someone's life, whether you did so instantaneously or over the course of a long period of servitude.

The brothers then had to work out what they were going to tell their father. They took Joseph's garment, stained it with the blood of a goat, and allowed Jacob to draw the natural conclusion (37:31–33). Notice that they did not actually lie to their father; they simply produced the robe and said, "Do you recognize this? Is it your son's robe?" Of course, there is a rich irony to Jacob being deceived by a garment and a dead goat, since those were exactly what he used to deceive his own father many years before (27:15–16).

Jacob then tore his garments and mourned for his son, refusing to be comforted by his other sons and daughters (37:34–35). This neatly demonstrates the problem behind the whole chapter: for Jacob, his other children did not count for much. It is as if Joseph had been his only son, so that with his death, Jacob's own life was over. It was not just Joseph's dreams that had been shattered by the events of that day. Jacob's dreams were destroyed as well.

Yet why was Jacob's world so completely overturned? One answer, of course, is his own favoritism of Joseph. Jacob had invested all of his hopes and dreams in this one son, the son of his old age. Remember, in calling him "the son of his old age," Jacob's love for Joseph was linked to Abraham's love for Isaac (Gen. 37:3; 21:2, 7). Jacob saw Joseph as the child through whom the Lord's promise of a messianic seed would be fulfilled. Now, with Joseph's apparent death, how would that promise be fulfilled? The dream that Jacob had stored up in his heart—Joseph's dream of the sun, moon, and stars coming and bowing down to him—was a dream that could not now be fulfilled. That is why Joseph's loss was not merely one of life's great storms for Jacob; it was a storm he could not weather. Yet at the same time, the narrator strikingly juxtaposes Jacob's intense grief with the announcement of Joseph's safe arrival in Egypt, where he was sold into Potiphar's house. Joseph's story was not yet over: he was not in Sheol, but merely down in Egypt, which was precisely where God's providential plan had brought him.

GOD'S SOVEREIGNTY OVER INEXPLICABLE EVENTS

The first and most obvious point to learn from this is God's sovereign control over all of our circumstances. This is a lesson that we will see repeatedly over the next few chapters of Genesis. Indeed, the lesson is repeated many times because we need to hear it repeatedly. God's sovereignty is at work in complex and profound ways throughout this story, just as it is in our own lives.

First, consider all of the "coincidences" that were necessary to get Joseph down to Egypt. To begin with, Jacob needed to send Joseph to check on his brothers. Joseph then had to meet the man who told him that the brothers had gone to Dothan. If the brothers had stayed in Shechem, Joseph could easily have found them, but then they wouldn't have been on the main camel route down to Egypt. What is more, even though Dothan was on the main camel route, days or perhaps weeks could pass without seeing one heading in the right direction. Reuben's plan to put Joseph in the pit, rather than kill him immediately, had to be accepted at first, but it also had to fail ultimately because Reuben was absent when the crucial discussion took place to sell Joseph. The passing caravan of Ishmaelites needed to be bound for Egypt, not some other destination, and they had to sell him into Potiphar's household, so that the pieces would be in place for the next part of God's plan. Finally, Jacob had to be successfully deceived by the brothers' ploy with the coat, or otherwise the family would surely have been irreparably ripped apart. All of these things needed to happen in exactly the right order at just the right time to get Joseph down to where he needed to be, so that ultimately he could save the entire family from famine. Coincidence? I don't think so.

At the same time, notice how confusing and painful many of these circumstances must have been for the people going through them. God was in sovereign control of everything, yet that sovereign control involved destroying the peace and happiness of both Jacob and Joseph. God's sovereign plan left Joseph stripped naked and thrown into a pit. His sovereign plan for the good of his family left Jacob inconsolably bereaved, in a state of sorrow and dark emptiness that would mark his life for the next twenty years or so. Jacob's and Joseph's dreams were completely shattered and broken, and there was no voice from heaven telling them it would all work out well in the end. They were left with nothing to fall back on, other than their faith in God and his promises: the hope that the God who brought Abraham's "child of his old age" back from the dead by substituting a ram for Isaac (Gen. 22:13–14), might somehow do the same thing here. That must have been a slender hope indeed, and I'm sure that there were plenty of times when Jacob's and Joseph's faith and hope gave way to doubt and despair.

Notice too that not even the most skilled counselor could have explained what on earth God was doing. It would take many years, and many more twists and turns in the story, before the necessity of these events could become clear. Yet at the end of the story, faith and hope are vindicated, while doubt and despair are vanquished.

That may be an encouraging thought for those wrestling with the bitter reality of God's painful providence. Perhaps you doubt whether God could possibly be in sovereign control of the mess that your life has become. Could it really be God who has made a shipwreck of your dreams? Or perhaps you believe that God is indeed in control, but you have become bitter and angry at the direction he has chosen to steer your life. You know that it is God who has shattered your dreams, and you are having a hard time dealing with that reality. Let Joseph's experience speak to you. Yes, God's sovereign providence does sometimes take us into and through storms that utterly shipwreck our hopes and dreams. God certainly doesn't promise an easy life of health and wealth for his followers. Yet it is precisely God's loving providence that is at work in these most painful of seasons. God is not capricious and mean, bringing painful circumstances into your life for no reason. He has profound lessons he wants to teach you and ways in which he will use you to glorify himself, which cannot be accomplished unless you pass through *this* storm. Joseph cannot save his people by staying comfortably at home. Jacob's idolatrous love for Joseph needs to be challenged, and for that to happen Joseph has to be taken away. God loves Jacob too much to let him comfortably hold on to his idolatry. So too, your pain is never meaningless: God always has a good purpose to accomplish through it, both in you and through you.

GOD'S SOVEREIGNTY OVER WILLFUL SIN

Second, God is sovereign over the brothers' willful sin. This is where many people balk at God's sovereignty. Certainly we affirm that God is sovereign over random circumstances like storms and natural disasters, but isn't human evil simply the result of human free will? Notice how necessary God's ordering of circumstances was for the brothers to act out their sinful impulses, however. As long as Joseph stayed safely at home, the brothers couldn't do anything about their hatred of him. The hatred in their hearts remained in seed form. In order for it to turn into attempted murder, there also needed to be an opportunity, which the events of this passage provided. If God had caused Jacob to think through the situation and keep Joseph at home, his brothers would never have had the

23

opportunity to sell Joseph into slavery, and the thoughts of their hearts might never have been fully revealed, even to themselves. Once God providentially provided the opportunity, the sins of their hearts emerged into the clear light of day.

It is the same way with our own painful personal experiences. We delight to tell the stories of the occasions when God has providentially kept us from harm. When terrorists attacked the Twin Towers in New York on 9/11, one woman was late for work because she met a famous actress on the sidewalk, which delayed her long enough that she hadn't arrived at work when the towers were hit. Surely God was in that "chance" encounter. Yet God was also sovereign over the sinful acts of the terrorists themselves—and is sovereign over our sins too. We have many sinful thoughts in our hearts on which we never act, simply because there is no opportunity to do so. Our hearts may be restrained from outward sin by the presence of other people, by the fear of being caught, by social taboos, and so on. That is the Lord's grace to us and to others: if we lived in a world where we all acted on every sinful idea in our hearts, we would truly be living in hell. For that reason, the Lord graciously restrains our hearts from outward sin in many different areas of our lives.

Yet at other times, for his own reasons, the Lord removes those restraints and puts us in a situation where we have both the motive and the opportunity to go ahead and sin, and our hearts are allowed to go where we want. Notice that in ordaining those circumstances, the Lord doesn't create our sin. He is never the author of our sinful deeds; our sinful deeds flow from our own hearts that truly want to sin. Yet the Lord is still sovereign over our sin by controlling all of the circumstances and shaping influences that bring us to the point where the seed of that particular sin in our hearts grows to the point of full flowering.

GOD'S GRACIOUS PURPOSE IN OUR SIN

When we sin, God may be graciously showing us what we are really capable of. We are easily deceived into thinking that we could never commit such and such a sin, especially if the Lord has surrounded us with many external restraints. If we come from a good family and church background, where we have been strongly encouraged by our circumstances to behave properly, we can easily believe that we are much better than people whose lives are marred by evident outward sin. Yet the reality is that if a particular sin is there in our thought lives—whether anger, lust, greed, malice, or whatever—all it would take are the right circumstances for that sin to bear its bitter fruit. For myself, I know that my relative purity as a teenager had very little to do with my sanctification and far more to do with God's gracious gift to me of social awkwardness and unattractiveness.

Alternatively, the Lord sometimes chooses to show us the sad truth about ourselves precisely by allowing us to live out the sin that is in our hearts. Only in this way will we truly understand our need for the gospel. One sin that the Lord chose not to restrain during my teenage years was a cutting and caustic tongue that used wit to build myself up by mocking and making fun of other people. That's a sinful habit I learned from my own family, where such skill was celebrated and applauded, and it is one with which I have struggled ever since. The words that I speak are a symptom of a proud heart that really thinks that I am better than the people that I mock. There are still plenty of times when I say hurtful things to people, which reminds me how little my heart has really changed in spite of all of God's grace to me, and therefore how much I still need the gospel. The sinful attitude is there, whether I say the words outwardly or not, of course, but I am far more likely to see the ugliness of my sin when the Lord allows those words to come out and I see something of the bitter fruit that my sin bears.

Perhaps the dream-shattering issue with which you are wrestling is the discovery that you are a much bigger sinner than you thought. It may be the same besetting sin that trips you up over and over again, or it might be a single dramatic fall into a sin that seems too great for God possibly to forgive you. If so, there is good news for you in this passage. Joseph's brothers planned to murder him, and then settled for selling him into lifelong slavery. These were not utter pagans, living their lives as strangers to God; they were the foundation stones of his people, the twelve patriarchs who would form the base on which God would build his holy people.

These are our spiritual ancestors too; we are no better than they were. We all sin and fall short of the glory of God daily, and if we are not guilty of the same specific outward sins, it is simply because God has providentially kept us from committing them, not because our hearts have never longed for them. It is not just terrorists and murderers who have broken God's law and deserve to face the consequences. We have all done the same thing, and we continue to follow the same patterns of death each and every day. Yet the amazing part of the story that God is writing throughout history is that we, like Joseph's brothers, can be included in the holy people God is calling to himself, the new Israel of God.

GOD'S PURSUIT OF OUR SHALOM

How is it possible for a holy God, whose eyes are too pure to look upon evil (Hab. 1:13), sovereignly to use our sin for his glory and for our good? The answer to that lies in the gospel, which is prefigured in striking ways in this chapter. God the Father sent his own beloved Son into this world to live among the descendants of Joseph's brothers to seek their *shalom*, their welfare. Unlike Jacob, this loving Father did so knowing exactly how it would turn out. In the parable of the tenants, Jesus told a story about the renters of a vineyard who abused and beat a series of messengers sent by the landlord. But when he sent his own son to them, they said, "This is the heir," and they took him and killed him (Matt. 21:33–41). Neither the Father nor the Son was surprised by the cross. Whereas God restrained Joseph's brothers from killing him, the Father did not restrain the sin of those who hated Jesus. He surrendered his precious Son into the hands of wicked men who stripped him, not of a royal robe, but of a simple peasant's garment, and then brutally beat him and executed him.

Commentators have pointed out Joseph's surprising silence after he meets his brothers.[2] In the earlier part of the chapter, Joseph is full of words: he brings a report to his father, he recounts his dreams, he responds "Here I am" when his father sends him to his brothers, and he explains his mission to the man in the field. But at the crucial point when his brothers seize him, this man of many words falls silent. In this too, he resembles Jesus: "Like a sheep that before its shearers is silent, so he opened not his mouth" (Isa. 53:7). The voice that could have commanded legions upon legions of angels to come and restrain those who were venting their sinful anger against him was silent. Jesus thus exercised his sovereignty even over his own death at the hands of wicked men. They had no power to commit such a sin against him, except the power that he himself gave them. Every breath with which they mocked him came from him. The strength in the arm that drove each nail into his flesh was strength that God himself had supplied. As Acts 2:23 puts it, Jesus was "crucified and killed by the hands of lawless men," but that very sinful act took place "according to the definite plan and foreknowledge of God."

But this Father's response to his Son's death was different from Jacob's response. Jacob believed that his eyes told him the whole story: Joseph was dead, and so were his dreams. God's plan to redeem humanity was over, destroyed by a freak accident. The forces of darkness and chaos had won. But the divine Father knew better. He knew that his Son's death was not the evidence that God's purpose had failed. Instead, it was the proof that divine love had triumphed. The bloodstained cross that told the story of Jesus' death would be the gateway to new life for millions upon untold millions of sinful men and women, who by it would be redeemed and given new hope.

At the cross, something happened that the men who nailed Jesus to it could never have anticipated, just as Joseph's brothers could never have anticipated what God was up to through their sinful and murderous jealousy. In *Les Misérables*, Fantine dreamed of a God who would be forgiving, and at the cross that dream was demonstrated to be a reality. The power of the cross lay precisely in the fact that the one who was being slain was sinless. He was not suffering for his own sin or dying for his own iniquity. He was not there by accident or against his will. He was there for us. In his death, we too died, and in his resurrection, we too were raised to new life. This gift of forgiveness comes to us freely, as we simply trust in what Jesus has done for us. Instead of trying to stand before God dressed in our own righteousness, justified by our own best efforts to do what is good and right, we put on the bloodstained robe of Jesus and ask God to recognize his Son's robe as our only claim to righteousness.

When we do that, in place of our own record of murderous anger, jealousy, pride, lust, covetousness, laziness, and the like, God gives us the perfect record of Jesus Christ. Jesus never entertained harsh thoughts against his brothers or said unkind words to the disciples or acted meanly toward others. His perfect love for his family is now credited to us as if it were our own, which is why broken and sinful people like Joseph's brothers—and you and me—can be forgiven and included in the family of faith. It is not about any righteousness that you and I can attain. It is solely based on his righteousness given to us, and his death that atones for all of our sins, both the ones that we act out and the ones that remain as seeds in our hearts.

This reality reshapes the way that you and I think about the terrible storms that still invade our lives, whether those storms come from our circumstances, from the painful sins that other people commit against us, or from the awful sins that we ourselves commit against others. How could a God who acts sovereignly in all circumstances and is even sovereign over the worst sinful acts of humans, *not* be at work for good in the storms of your life? He may be at work in painful ways; he will not always restrain the sins of others against you, nor your sins against others. Our dreams for this world may be shattered, but only so that God can bring something purer and richer out of the broken pieces. As the psalmist put it, "Weeping may tarry for the night, but joy comes with the morning" (Ps. 30:5). God will use our painful trials, our sins, and the sins of others to show us more about our hearts, more about our need of him, more about our desperate need of the gospel, more about the brokenness of the fallen world in which we live. He will use these trials to refine and sanctify us and to teach us to focus more on the true treasure that we must seek, which is him and him alone.

FOR FURTHER REFLECTION

1. What were Joseph's and Jacob's dreams? How did those dreams impact their relationships with Jacob's other sons?

2. What are, or have been, your dreams? Has your pursuit of those dreams led you to treat others sinfully? When your hopes have been dashed by circumstance, have you clung to your dreams or to God's promises?

3. God worked salvation through the sinful crucifixion of Jesus. How does that transform your understanding of God's purposes in your own sins and in the sins of others against you? Are there positive results that can flow from sin?

CHAPTER THREE

A BREAKTHROUGH FOR VICTIMS AND SINNERS (GENESIS 38)

D ysfunction, death, sex, blame shifting, prostitution, incest, a paternity scandal: it all sounds like titillating tabloid headlines. But in Genesis 38, the all-too-familiar cycle from our modern news sources plays out in ancient history upon the pages of Scripture. There we find scandal and fallout, sin and consequences, complete with bitter repercussions in the lives of those directly involved and collateral damage in those around them. Many lives are forever changed for ill. Is there any hope for them in the aftermath of sin?

Closer to home, we face the same question. Similar story lines play out among friends and family. Sometimes they have headline-grabbing potential. At other times, the life-sapping impact of evil is more subtle and insidious. In our own lives, many of us experience the fallout from the wrong that we have done or that has been done to us. Is there any hope for us in the aftermath of sin?

Yes, there is—but it may look very different from our expectations. The grittiness of this passage helpfully puts to death some of our worst tendencies in reading the Bible.

We often approach the Bible as if it were a series of heart-warming stories designed to inspire us to good, clean, moral living. In its place, we find a far more profound hope. This disturbing passage moves beyond the ravages of sin to provide a picture of hope, transformation, and divine breakthrough for Judah and Tamar. It is the story of God triumphing over the evil in and among us. Sometimes God triumphs through harnessing our evil thoughts, words, and actions for purposes we had never intended.

JUDAH'S JUNK

We have already observed that the story of Joseph is really the story of his whole family, a family torn apart by favoritism, arrogance, envy, hatred, conspiracy, and lies. Following the sale of Joseph into slavery in Egypt, chapter 38 opens ominously with another step in the dissolution of the family. After Joseph's involuntary departure, Judah voluntarily leaves his brothers. The "going down" of Judah echoes the "going down" of Joseph to Egypt (compare Genesis 38:1 to 39:1). God had promised Abraham that his family would become a great nation and a blessing to all nations. But just three generations in, the family was unraveling. Judah was simply not interested in being part of God's plan.

Why was that? Judah's experience of life in his family had been anything but a shower of blessings. Instead, he had been the recipient of a lot of junk. He was the fourth son of Leah, the unwanted and unloved wife. Grandfather Laban had resorted to trickery to unload her onto Jacob, and Jacob showed her little love or affection. At the end of Genesis 29, we learn that Judah's very name, "This time I will praise the Lord," seemed to mark the (temporary) end of Leah's vain efforts to win Jacob's affection through the bearing of sons. In Genesis 33, the second-rate status of Leah and her sons is reinforced as Jacob makes his personal pecking order cruelly obvious. Worried about a violent reception by his brother Esau, Jacob uses Leah and her sons as human shields to facilitate an escape for Rachel and Joseph, if that should become necessary. Imagine the question coming from the back seat of Leah's camel: "Mom, why are they so far behind us?" Even after Joseph was presumed dead, Jacob's blatant favoritism continued in his excessive mourning. Jacob refused to find any comfort in his other children, as if they counted for nothing. Judah had some significant relational and emotional baggage.

A FRESH START

Rather than be a second-class citizen in a family of blessing, Judah struck out on his own for a fresh start. It is hard to fault his choice. Would you choose to remain with this dysfunctional family? Would you want to stick around a father like Jacob, if you were anyone other than Joseph? Surely Judah had suffered enough humiliation and indignity. With varying degrees of success, many of us have likewise tried to make our own clean break with our past for precisely these reasons: "I just want to get away from this family . . . or these friends . . . or this town." College students see education and success as their keys to freedom and independence. Young professionals move to the big city as a way of escape. In certain circumstances, moving away from an unhealthy situation may be wise and necessary, especially when recommended by godly, biblical counselors.

However, the problem is that Judah was not just turning his back on his family, but also on God and his promises. Judah's immersion among the Canaanites, where he found himself a close friend, a wife, and some neighbors, was exactly what Abraham and Isaac feared for their family. In the land of promise, the family of blessing constantly faced the temptation of mixing, assimilating, and becoming indistinguishable from their pagan surroundings. Such assimilation threatened to bring Israel under the judgment of God for participating in the false worship, social evils, and personal wickedness of their neighbors. This is the very process that unfolded later in Israel's history, in the time of the judges. Indeed, after leaving his family, Judah rapidly became enmeshed in false worship, personal wickedness, and social evils.

Yet Judah's problem was not merely that he imbibed wrong attitudes and ideas from his Canaanite neighbors. The clean-break approach didn't just fail because Judah chose the wrong new situation. The main hitch with the clean-break approach is that you cannot make a clean break with yourself. We have already seen that Judah possessed superior leadership skills, which he used not to protect and lead his brothers but to orchestrate the profitable disposal of Joseph. And as Judah's fresh-start family imploded, he was perpetuating and exacerbating the same old pathologies he learned from his father, Jacob.

INHERITED BAGGAGE

Jacob's sex life operated in overdrive as he juggled relationships with four women. Likewise, Judah lacked sexual restraint. He did not exactly romance his wife; he saw her and took her (Gen. 38:2)—language that is suggestive of lustful desire and transgression elsewhere in Genesis. Eve saw and took the forbidden fruit (3:6). The flood was precipitated by the sons of God seeing and taking the daughters of men (6:2). So also, Pharaoh saw and took Sarah (12:15), and Shechem took Dinah (34:2). Like his father, Jacob, Judah was a failure as a faithful lover and husband.

As a parent, Judah was disengaged and distant. Suggestive of Judah's rejection of the God of his fathers, he named his firstborn son Er, which is "evil" written backward in

Hebrew.[1] Although Judah named his firstborn, his wife named his second and third sons, Onan and Shelah. So also, Jacob's wives, rather than Jacob, named nearly all their children. In contrast, the previous generations were marked by the fatherly participation of Abraham and Isaac in the naming process (Gen. 16:15; 21:3; 25:25–26). While the Hebrew is ambiguous, Judah may have been in an entirely different town when Shelah was born—the town of Chezib, which some scholars translate as "city of lies."[2] Deceit was a consistent feature of the Abrahamic family, and, as we shall see, it came to the fore in Judah's dealings with Tamar, the wife of Er. Fifteen or twenty years later, the fallout of Judah's parental failure continued. Two of his grown sons, Er and Onan, were deemed so evil by God that he struck them dead. The last time that God had put people to death in Genesis was when he destroyed Sodom and Gomorrah, and this is the first time in Scripture that such a judgment is rendered against specific individuals.

So much for Judah's hope for a fresh start. By the time the dust settled, Judah had lost two of his three sons, and his entire family line was in jeopardy. Judah was stuck. According to the conventions of the age, it was his duty to give his last remaining son, Shelah, to his widowed daughter-in-law, Tamar. But Tamar's marriage partners were 0-for-2 in the category of staying alive (she had been given to Onan after Er died, but Onan died soon thereafter). So Judah stalled for time and told Tamar to go back to her father's house, thereby shirking his responsibility to take care of her. However, Judah's insincere ruse still left the survival of the family in jeopardy, because he could not acquire a different wife for Shelah without admitting that his son was old enough to fulfill his obligation to Tamar.

The junk just kept piling up. At first, a lot of it had been dumped on Judah, but now he was the one dishing it out to everyone around him. By the end of the first part of the story, in verse 11, most of it is getting dumped on Tamar.

It is curious logic: Judah sold his own brother, ditched his family, plunged into a shotgun wedding, ran with the wrong crowd, and ignored his children. However, he was sure that those two mounds of fresh dirt that used to be his sons were Tamar's fault.

The level of Judah's self-deception and blindness is both astonishing and frightening. It is astonishing because, as outside observers, we can see that he is so clearly in the wrong. But it is also frightening because we so naturally do the same thing. Like Judah, we are prone to live in cities of lies—distorted versions of reality, overlaid with a thin layer of our own innocence and self-exoneration. All of us suffer. At some point, we all also suffer from the actions of other people. But what so often happens next is that a legitimate reflex goes into overdrive. It is good to be able to understand that some of the evil that happens to us is outside of our control; we are being impacted by the sin of others. Our ability to make a distinction between things that are our own fault and things that come from others is a learned skill. Often children do not yet have that skill. As a result, when something bad happens, such as their parents getting divorced, they assume that they themselves are somehow responsible. However, having recognized that we sometimes suffer because of someone else's sin, we can twist that knowledge in order to find ways to blame all of our suffering on other people. We can become blind to our own guilt, and that blindness can make the harmful effects of our own sin against others even worse.

TAMAR'S TRAP

In Judah's case, his junk and his blindness tightened the noose of Tamar's trap. In the ancient world, people often married shortly after puberty, so she was probably still quite young, perhaps still a teenager. Consider what this young girl had experienced. Her first husband was struck down by God, which left her a very young widow. Tamar's second sexual partner, Onan, abused what was supposed to be a duty of kindness and provision for her. The practice of levirate marriages was intended to perpetuate the memory and the family line of the deceased husband who died childless, and to alleviate the poverty of the widow, who would then be provided for in advanced age (Deut. 25:5–6). But if Onan raised up a child for his brother Er, that child would inherit the blessings promised to the firstborn, not him. To maintain his new position of privilege, he was willing to erase the legacy and memory of his brother in a way sadly reminiscent of the violent jealousy of Joseph's brothers.

Even worse, Onan turned familial duty into an opportunity to exploit Tamar. If Onan had no intention of fathering children to take Er's place, there was no reason to engage in intercourse at all. But Onan used the defenseless Tamar for his personal sexual gratification. The word "whenever" in verse 9 highlights the fact that Onan's behavior was repeated and regular. So Tamar's second sexual partner was struck dead, leaving her a widow twice over and still childless. She had been privately shamed by the sexual abuse of Onan, and publicly shamed by the growing perception, perhaps encouraged by Judah, that she was cursed. If Judah would not keep his promise to Tamar to give her to Shelah, she would remain in that unwanted condition, at the very lowest level of society. The irony of her name highlights the cruel twist of her fate. Tamar means "palm tree," an image of beauty. This young, attractive girl, who once was full of hope for the future, had become damaged goods in her own thinking, as well as in public opinion. She was yet another victim of the sins of the members of God's chosen family, sins that turned life in the family of blessing into a trap of suffering and shame.

Many of us today suffer from the same sort of shame as Tamar. Single women are still at tremendous risk of descending into poverty, especially if divorced or widowed.

One in every four women and one in every six men experience sexual abuse. As in Tamar's case, these situations are often caused or exacerbated by parents, family members, or fellow Christians. Many people are deeply touched by terrible circumstances that leave them feeling like damaged goods. Many have been betrayed by those who were supposed to protect them.

TAMAR'S TRICK

As time passed, Tamar decided that she was not content to stay trapped in her circumstances. When it became more and more obvious that Judah had no intention of fulfilling his promise, Tamar set her own trap for him. If Judah was going to deceive her, she could deceive him too. After all, that was the family way.

It is remarkable how easily Tamar's trickery worked. Judah's sexual appetite was apparently a matter of common knowledge. He headed out on a business trip at sheep-shearing time, the cultural equivalent of student trips to Florida on spring break. Tamar seemed to know that all she had to do was to be there and be available. She smoothly played the part of a prostitute and negotiated for Judah to leave his signet, cord, and staff until payment was made (Gen. 38:18). In this, Tamar secured the ancient equivalent of Judah's wallet, complete with driver's license and credit cards. This is exactly what Tamar wanted: something to identify Judah. Ironically, this took place at a location identified as "the entrance to Enaim" (38:14), which literally translates as "the opening of the eyes." Though Judah was blind to Tamar's identity and his own continuing blindness and hypocrisy, the consequences of their encounter would ultimately open his eyes.

In many ways, Tamar was an innocent victim of the sins of Judah and his family. Given the cultural convention of the time, she may not even have had a say in whether she wanted to join this family. The trap she laid for Judah was about her getting justice and righting a wrong. Yet, at the same time, her trap was highly risky, not to mention highly questionable ethically, morally, and legally. She was intentionally engaging in prostitution to entrap Judah. Their relationship as father-in-law and daughter-in-law raises the issue of incest. As a result, the text emphasizes that Judah did not knowingly sleep with his daughter-in-law (Gen. 38:15), and that they did not have further sexual encounters after this incident (38:26). Tamar set out to right a wrong, but she did it in a profoundly disturbing way.

As it was with Judah, so it was with Tamar. When we suffer at the hands of others, no one remains fully innocent. Theologian Miroslav Volf writes,

> There is an intertwining of victim and violator through the very nature of violation. The violence ensnares the psyche of the victim, propels its action in the form of defensive reaction, and . . . robs it of innocence. By denying the reality of absolute innocence, we are clearly not suggesting that we should blame the victim for being victimized. Instead, this draws attention to one of the most insidious aspects of the practice of evil. In addition to inflicting harm, the practice of evil keeps re-creating a world without innocence. Evil generates new evil as evildoers fashion victims in their own ugly image.[3]

When we are wronged, we respond wrongly. We may lack Judah's position of authority to enforce oppression or Tamar's audacity to fight back. Yet in our minds we can still wage war against those who have hurt us, by nursing bitterness, harboring resentment, and reveling in their sufferings and failings. We continue the cycle of sin and counter-sin. Where then is the hope? Is there any way to break the cycle of sufferers turned sinners and victims turned perpetrators?

JUDAH'S BREAKTHROUGH

There is indeed hope, but it does not come from anyone already caught up in the cycle. Someone from outside has to break in and arrest the cycle of sinful action and reaction. Appropriately enough, our story ends with the birth of twins, one of whom is called Perez, which means "breach" or "breakthrough." Likewise, the personal stories end with twin breakthroughs for Judah and Tamar.

The occasion for Judah's breakthrough began with a rumor. The ESV footnotes are helpful to convey the import of this rumor: Tamar has *prostituted* herself and is pregnant *by prostitution*. That report provided the opportunity for all of the junk to come spilling out of Judah's heart as he says, "Bring her out and burn her" (see Gen. 38:24). Notice how Judah jumped at this chance to get rid of Tamar. He was still blaming her for everything that had gone wrong. He was delighted at the opportunity to dispose of her, which meant that Shelah could finally get married. The dilemma would be resolved, and the family might survive. Best of all, Tamar could be condemned as a slut, and Judah could position himself as the fine, upstanding member of the community. Yet Judah remained completely blind to his own sin and hypocrisy. Judah had been with a prostitute just three months earlier. His companion, Hirah, and the residents of Enaim all knew that.

Amazingly, even in Judah's self-righteous hypocrisy, God showed him mercy. It came through a simple message to Judah from Tamar: "I'm pregnant by the man who owns these. Please identify them" (see Gen. 38:25). The light went on, and Judah, staring at his own personal belongings, finally saw the truth: "She is more righteous than I" (Gen. 38:26). After years of blaming everyone else for his problems, Judah recognized his own guilt. He had lied to Tamar, denying her rights and leaving her without any recourse. He was quite literally guilty of the same sin for which he wanted her killed. Under later biblical law, both deserved death (Deut. 22:21–22). However, what she had done out of desperation, he had done only to satisfy his desires. At the same time, the irrefutable evidence of his own guilt was also the irrefutable evidence of the lie that he had believed about Tamar. It was not her fault that her past partners had all perished. She was not cursed. He was the living proof.

But it was not just Judah's relationship to Tamar that was transformed. Her words, "Please identify these," parallel exactly what he and his brothers had said to Jacob when they brought him Joseph's bloodied coat (Gen. 38:25; 37:32). If there is one thing Judah gained from all of the painful experiences and losses that he suffered, it was a greater sympathy for his father. Now Judah knew from personal experience what it was like to lose sons. Like Jacob, he tried to protect his youngest, even to the hurt of others. He too had been duped by a mysterious, veiled woman into a different relationship from the one he had expected. Jacob did not recognize Leah, and Judah failed to recognize Tamar. Judah's confrontation with the depths of his own sin fostered reconciliation with his brothers and especially with his father. He finally saw how very much like his father he had become.

As the rest of the story unfolds, we will see how pivotal was the change wrought in Judah. The events of Genesis 38 probably stretched out over twenty to twenty-two years, a period of time that matched the time that Joseph spent in Egypt in chapters 39–42. The two stories are essentially running in parallel, so that Judah's confession of guilt to Tamar probably occurred shortly before the events of chapter 43. In those subsequent events, a chastened Judah showed compassion to his father, understanding Jacob's hurt, and pledged that he himself would accept the blame if he failed to bring Benjamin safely home to his father. He employed his natural abilities as a leader to save the family.

Unless we have our eyes opened, we will remain as blind as Judah was. As Volf writes,

> Perpetrators tirelessly generate their own innocence, and do so by the double strategy of denying the wrongdoing [I did not do it!] and re-interpreting the moral significance of their actions [I couldn't help it! She asked for it!] . . . And this same double denial is the stuff out of which the peculiar blend of fraud and self-deception is concocted, by which individuals seek to evade being held responsible for evildoing.[4]

Isn't that exactly what we do? We tell outright lies or we spin the truth to our advantage, to maintain our right and our innocence. What is truly frightening is having this pointed out, and then starting to listen to oneself. It is truly amazing how naturally blame shifting and denial spring to our lips. "I was tired. I was not at my best. If only you hadn't said it in that way." We are trapped in denial and self-deception, to which we are blinded.

OPENING OUR EYES

But the story of Judah is also the story of "Enaim," the opening of our eyes. In the Gospels, time and time again, Jesus gives sight to the blind. God is the one who reveals himself to us and reveals to us who we really are. When we go out from a darkened room on a sunny day, the first shafts of light can be piercing and painful; so too, confrontation with our sin may shock us and scare us. We did not know we had something like that in us! It may hurt our pride, and it certainly embarrasses us. Think of how it must have been for Judah. A few weeks earlier, he had given up trying to recover his most important personal belongings for fear that he would be mocked by the residents of Enaim. Halting Tamar's public burning because he was revealed as the father would have been far more embarrassing. However, there is no other way to learn humility than by being confronted with the embarrassing, shameful, foolish, hurtful, sinful things we do. We might as well get used to it, because humility is very important to God, and he seems intent on working this part of the mind of Christ in us.

However, the other amazing thing to which Judah's broken and rebuilt life points us is that we don't need to be crushed by our sin. Having our eyes opened, so that we see the wrong that we do and the hurt that we cause, can be incredibly demoralizing. My wife and I often feel exhausted and dispirited after yet another fight over an utterly meaningless issue. Why can't we figure out our problems, while being kind to one another and keeping things in perspective? The answer is that there may be some very good reason why God wants us both acquainted with our prickly defensiveness, the shortness of our tempers, and our overweening desire for complete affirmation. In fact, there may be things that God has for us to do in the future that we could not do without those experiences and rebukes.

The story of Judah reminds us of Jesus' words to bold, confident Peter, right before his fall: "When you have turned again, strengthen your brothers" (Luke 22:32). Just as Jesus had a purpose in Peter's denial and restoration, so he had a purpose in Judah's twenty years of self-deception and blindness. God had something positive that he purposed to accomplish in and through Judah. God can, and does, crack the hardest of hearts. God can, and does, reclaim the biggest of sinners. The improbable repentance of Judah is incredibly good news because all of us are much bigger sinners than we imagine, with much harder hearts than we realize.

TAMAR'S BREAKTHROUGH

Tamar's breakthrough is equally glorious. One moment, having compromised her innocence in an extremely risky bid for her rights, she was headed for the flames as a condemned prostitute. The next moment, she was cleared by Judah's confession: "She is more righteous than I!" The family disgrace—the girl who brought bad luck to everyone with whom she came into contact—was welcomed back into the family. This reversal is anticipated by an earlier wordplay in the conversations between Judah and Hirah. When Judah first saw the disguised Tamar, he assumed her to be a prostitute (Gen. 38:15). The same charge was leveled against her later (38:24). But Hirah and the residents of Enaim assumed that she was a "cult prostitute" (38:21–22). Hirah may have been trying either to describe the situation more accurately, based upon Tamar's use of the veil, or to soften the awkwardness of the situation for his friend Judah. Ritual prostitution was certainly one of the entrenched evils that eventually brought God's wrath upon the Canaanites. But in this story, the insertion of the different term "cult prostitute," a Hebrew euphemism that literally means "holy woman," points to the coming reversal of Tamar's judicial, social, and spiritual position.

Tamar's breakthrough also placed her in the very middle of God's saving purposes for all humanity. The birth of Tamar's twins echoed the earlier birth of twins back in Genesis 25. Like Esau, Zerah was remembered by his association with something red at birth (Gen. 38:30; 25:25). Perez, whose name means "breakthrough," sneaked out in front of his brother, much as his grandfather Jacob had done. The special divine blessing of twins is one of the early hints that the family of Judah will be the line of promise through the children of Tamar. Later in Scripture, Tamar appears at two crucial points. At the wedding of Ruth and Boaz, the elders prayed, "May your house be like the house of Perez, whom Tamar bore to Judah" (Ruth 4:12). Once thought cursed, Tamar's memory was now invoked as a model of God's blessing. Through Boaz, a descendant of her son Perez, Tamar was thus an ancestor of King David. Centuries later, Tamar appeared again in Matthew's genealogy as a woman in the line of Jesus (Matt. 1:3). Tamar had faced a hopeless future at the bottom of society—a childless, abused, discarded widow. However, through God's intervention, she became a mother of the Messiah.

What an incredible picture this is of God's intervening grace. We are all damaged goods, profoundly broken. Yet that is why Jesus came! Jesus is the breakthrough son, who came to seek and to save that which is lost. The Son of God personally stepped into history and chose to be born into the sort of family that would grab tabloid headlines. Through Judah and Tamar, Jesus was the son of a sinner and a prostitute. Indeed, he spent much of his time on earth with sinners and prostitutes, telling them joyfully about the triumph of grace over our just moral desserts. He brought grace, acceptance, transformation, and hope for sinning sufferers and victim-perpetrators. Jesus inverted what Judah had first done to Tamar. While Judah had blamed Tamar for his sins to maintain his own innocence, Jesus took our blame and our shame, so that it might be put to death with him at the cross. He now covers us with his perfection, saying, "You are righteous," taking away our sins and making us acceptable to his Father. In that way, he removes our curse forever and welcomes us safely into the family of God, where we can be loved and protected by him.

FOR FURTHER REFLECTION

1. How was Judah sinned against? How did he respond to the sins of others against him?

2. How was Tamar sinned against? How did she respond to the sins of others against her?

3. Have you struggled with sexual sin? Have you sexually abused others or been sexually abused? How have you responded?

4. How did God break through the cycle of sin in Judah's family? Do you struggle to believe that God can break through the cycle of sin in your life?

5. What grace did God show to Judah? What legacy did he give to Judah?

6. What grace did God show to Tamar? What legacy did he give to Tamar?

CHAPTER FOUR

GOD'S WONDERFUL PLAN (GENESIS 39)

We've probably all heard the statement, "God loves you and has a wonderful plan for your life." But then the realities of life press in on us relentlessly: sickness, pain, broken relationships, abuse, shattered dreams, temptation, sin, death. So where is this wonderful plan for my life? What on earth is God up to? That's actually a great question. When we explore what God is up to in our lives, we discover that his good plan is not a plan for our ease and comfort, but rather a plan for our death and resurrection—dying to sin and to our old self, and rising to a whole new life in him. He loves you and me too much to leave us unchanged. This process is often hard and painful, as Joseph discovered, and the pathway along which you are called to walk may be similarly confusing and disorienting. Yet along that difficult pathway, Joseph found that the Lord was with him, even when he felt most abandoned and alone. In the light of Joseph's experience in Egypt, we too may discover that even when God's wonderful plan leads us into trials and temptation, his grace is sufficient for us.

47

GOD'S WONDERFUL PLAN FOR JOSEPH

Joseph must have grown up hearing a great deal about God's wonderful plan for his life. He was the favorite son in a favored family. The Lord had called his great-grandfather, Abraham, to be the father of his chosen people, the one through whom blessing would come to all nations (Gen. 12:1–3). His own father, Jacob, had been chosen to be the heir of that blessing in an oracle given before he was even born (25:22–23). However, Jacob's pathway to receiving this blessing was long and convoluted, complicated by his own sin and the sin of others against him.

Now Joseph in turn was the favored son, born of Jacob's favored wife, Rachel, and protected and pampered by his father from his earliest days. The richly ornamented coat that he wore was a symbol of his high status in the family. And this was not just his father's wonderful plan for his life. While Joseph was still a young man, the Lord sent him two dreams in which he was at the center. In the first dream, his brother's sheaves bowed down to him while they were out harvesting in the field, while in the second dream the entire universe—sun, moon, and stars—came bowing down to him. If anyone ever had a reason for saying, "God loves me and has a wonderful plan for my life," surely it was Joseph.

GOD'S PLAN DERAILED?

Then everything in Joseph's life seemed to go horribly wrong. His father sent him to visit his brothers while they were out watching the sheep (Gen. 37:14). When his brothers saw him coming in the distance, they conspired to kill him (37:18). Only when some Midianite traders happened to pass by did they revise their plan into a money-making scheme (37:28). They sold Joseph to these traders, who took him down to Egypt, where he was purchased by an

Egyptian official named Potiphar (37:36). God's wonderful plan for Joseph's life seemed shattered by a combination of human jealousy and greed. Where was God at the crucial moments of Joseph's life when his dreams were being derailed? Joseph must surely have pondered that question many times on the way down to Egypt and during his days as a household slave.

Yet the narrator, who is remarkably reticent about identifying God's role in the rest of Joseph's story, breaks in to inform us no fewer than five times in the opening five verses of Genesis 39 that the Lord was with Joseph in Egypt, giving him success and causing him to find favor with his new employer. He wants to make sure that you don't miss the point that just because life is hard and isn't turning out the way that you hoped, that doesn't mean God is against you or that his wonderful plan for your life has been derailed. God can be with you in Egypt, in bondage, and in a set of frustrating circumstances where you are experiencing the consequences of other people's sins against you, just as much as he is with you in the sunnier days in Canaan, where everything seemed to be going according to (your) plan. In fact, Joseph began to embody the Abrahamic promise of being a blessing to the nations precisely in that situation of trial and loss: everything that his Egyptian master entrusted to him prospered for Joseph's sake (Gen. 39:5). According to verse 3, Potiphar recognized what was going on: he saw that the Lord was with Joseph. Joseph's painful "sidetrack" turned out to be a wonderful opportunity for this particular Egyptian to see the Lord at work.

Perhaps you can relate to this. You may be dealing with a difficult and challenging situation in your life: you are experiencing painful trials that have radically changed your prospects for the future and condemned you to a life you would never have chosen for yourself. What is God doing? Perhaps he will use your suffering to bring you into contact with someone who needs to see the Lord at work.

It may be a fellow patient or a nurse or doctor at the cancer clinic, or perhaps a neighbor or friend who is watching you endure your trial. Maybe there is someone near you who needs to see what "the Lord is with us" looks like in the midst of suffering, pain, and loss. It is one thing to declare that "the Lord is with us" when there isn't a cloud in your sky. It is quite another to be able to confess that "the Lord is with us" in the valley of deep shadow.

THE RISE AND FALL OF JOSEPH

Yet the twists and turns in the Lord's plans for Joseph were by no means finished.

Joseph became manager of Potiphar's household, which represented a meteoric rise for a slave (Gen. 39:4). So far everything follows the storyline that we would like to believe: serve God and everything will go well for you. You will be blessed and so will everyone around you. Even if you have to go through difficulties, your trials will only be temporary and will issue in new and exciting opportunities to share the gospel. You may get sick, but God will heal you and make it all better. One relationship may be broken or destroyed, but a new and better one waits around the corner. Isn't that what it means for God to be with us?

Joseph's story shows us a different view of reality. As rapidly as the ship of Joseph's fortunes rose, it equally swiftly hit a rock and was wrecked. Joseph found himself right back at the bottom of the heap again, in an Egyptian jail (Gen. 39:20). Worse, this twist of fortunes did not come because of moral failure on Joseph's part. Rather, it was his faithful obedience to God, the very thing which had apparently caused his rise, which now also caused his fall.

The story of how it happened is familiar. Joseph was a good-looking man, a family trait he shared with his grandmother, Sarah, and his mother, Rachel (Gen. 12:11; 29:17). Potiphar's wife noticed his attractiveness and desired him (39:7). The temptation that presented itself to Joseph was sudden, real, and direct. This story is a lot more like an attempted rape than a seduction. After all, Joseph is the beautiful one, not Potiphar's wife, and she doesn't allure him with honeyed words. She simply commanded Joseph, "Come to bed with me!" (39:7 NIV). It was not a request; it was a demand. It was spoken in the same tone of voice that she would use in telling him to straighten the chairs or dust the furniture. He was the slave; she was the mistress. This is the temptation that comes when someone in power over you tells you to deny your beliefs or suffer the consequences. It may be an employer who threatens to fire you or an abusive family member who will subject you to physical or emotional hurt if you don't do what he says.

In such a situation, it would have been easy for Joseph to rationalize sinful compliance as the only viable option. To give in would have been easy and self-protective; to refuse would almost certainly have negative repercussions. After all, hell hath no fury like a woman scorned. But Joseph did not comply. He explained to Potiphar's wife that it would be a betrayal of the trust placed in him by Potiphar, and he went on to the deeper and more important reason why he could not do it: it would be a sin against God (Gen. 39:9).

Bringing God into the picture shows Joseph's aware-ness of the Lord's presence with him, even in this nearly impossible situation. He did not put his faith to one side when faced with the challenges of living in "the real world." Instead, when he reckoned up the balance sheet, he saw clearly that the choice that faced him in that instant was between satisfying his employer's wife by offending God and satisfying God by offending his employer's wife. He made the right choice, not just once or twice, but repeatedly as she confronted him day after day (Gen. 39:10).

THE SECRET OF JOSEPH'S SUCCESS

How was Joseph able to do that, when we so often fail and fall in the face of much lesser temptations? Sometimes we successfully say no to a temptation the first time around and the second time and even the third time, but sooner or later Satan wears us down with his persistence. Not so with Joseph. Yet there is no grand secret to defeating temptation here. Certainly, Joseph tried his hardest to avoid situations of temptation by not being alone with Potiphar's wife. Yet such an approach merely deals with external factors, not the heart. However careful you are, sooner or later temptation will come at you in some form or another.

Ultimately, Joseph's only defense against sin was a heart that wanted to please God more than to experience pleasure or avoid pain. That's our real problem. My difficult circumstances don't make me sin. The other people who invite me to join them in wrongdoing don't make me sin. My own heart draws me into sin because it wants something more than it wants to please God. James poses the question, "What causes quarrels and what causes fights among you?" (James 4:1). The answer is not the impossible people that you live with or the trying circumstances that surround you.[1] The problem is that we want something more than we want God. Why do I get angry when I struggle to write a sermon, and on Friday night all I have is a pile of empty words? It is not because I care so much about my congregation's spiritual needs and am tenderly afraid for their souls. I wish it were so, but it isn't. It is because I don't want to have to get up early on Saturday and rewrite the whole thing. I'd rather lie in bed. It is because I am afraid that it will still be a pile of empty words on Sunday morning, and no one will go away impressed by my preaching ability. My self-centered and proud heart has its own wonderful plan for my life, a plan that doesn't involve temptation, struggle, and suffering—a plan in which everyone bows down and glorifies me. I want to think that preaching is a skill for which I can take the credit. I resent being reminded that I am merely a messenger boy who is utterly dependent on God for anything meaningful to say.

It is the same for you. Whatever sin you struggle with, whether it is pride, lust, gossip, overeating, or anything else, its power comes from the fact that you want something more than you want God, and that sin seems to offer you a way to get it. If Joseph had valued his safety, comfort, and position in the house more than he loved God, he would have given in to Potiphar's wife. It is as simple as that.

RESISTING SIN

At least, giving in to sin is as simple as that. Resisting sin is an entirely different story. If the problem is with our hearts and not our circumstances, then resisting sin will require more than simply staying at a distance from tempting situations. It will require a change in our hearts, which is something we cannot do for ourselves. We cannot simply decide to turn over a new leaf and just stop sinning; we need to be given a new heart with new desires. If there is one lesson to be learned from the experience of Old Testament Israel, it is this: having God's perfect law and a powerful experience of God's deliverance is not enough. As the Lord reminded Israel through the prophets, they needed new hearts (Jer. 31:33; Ezek. 36:26). Ultimately, the reason why Joseph was able to say no to such a powerful temptation was the work of God. Just as the presence of God with Joseph enabled him to prosper in everything he did for Potiphar, so too it was because the Lord was with him that he was able to say, "How can I do such a thing and sin against God?" That thought did not come from himself; it came from God.

The Lord was sovereign over every aspect of Joseph's life. God's plan for Joseph's life included temptation, so he orchestrated the circumstances that exposed Joseph to it in a powerful form. He could easily have made sure that Potiphar and his wife were happily married, or that Joseph had been born ugly. Yet he did not do so, because part of Joseph's story included facing and resisting temptation. God brought him into this temptation and, in this case, brought him through unscathed.

THE CHARGE AGAINST JOSEPH

Yet doing the right thing did not solve Joseph's problem. Day after day, the same temptation confronted him, and though he did his best to avoid it—he refused even to be with her in the house (Gen. 39:10)—it was always there. Finally, Potiphar's wife made one last try. She waited until she could catch him alone, grabbed his cloak, and commanded him again, "Come to bed with me!" (39:12 NIV). With that kind of in-your-face temptation, there was only one thing to do: run for your life. So Joseph fled, leaving his outer garment behind (39:13). Not for the first time in his life, he found his own clothing used against him. His brothers had used his fancy coat to convince his father he had been killed by a wild animal. Now his cloak was used by Potiphar's wife as the evidence that he had assaulted her.

Potiphar was left with the unenviable choice of siding with a slave and exposing his wife as a liar or getting rid of Joseph. He chose the latter course, though the fact that he merely had Joseph thrown in prison suggests that he did not entirely believe his wife's story. The normal punishment for such an offense would have been immediate execution.[2] That was probably cold comfort to Joseph, who found himself in prison, at rock bottom once again, falsely accused and judged guilty of a terrible crime. It is surely at this point that the second, harder temptation came to Joseph: the temptation to feel abandoned by God. After all, he had done the right thing. He had resisted temptation, but the Lord, far from protecting him, stood by and let a great injustice be done. Where is God when you really need him?

Of course, such circumstances reveal the truth about our hearts. If we are doing the right thing because we think that that will earn God's favor or will force him to give us what we really want, then when our "faithfulness" doesn't seem to be working for us, we will grow resentful, bitter, and angry. If we are obeying God to get something from him in return, then that something really controls our hearts, not God. Perhaps you think that if you tithe faithfully, God really ought to make your business prosper, or that if you make and keep a commitment to sexual purity, God owes you a spouse. Often, our obedience to God's law is not about pleasing him at all. It is about trying to use God to get what we really want. The truth is revealed whenever God does not give us what we want: our anger and resentment reveal what we are really serving God for. Like the elder brother in the story of the Prodigal Son (Luke 15:25–32), we may have obeyed scrupulously without ever really having loved. Our obedience was actually about serving our own pride and furthering the image of ourselves as the righteous and obedient one in the family.

GOD AT WORK

Yet for Joseph there seems to have been no such resentment and anger. Even though he found himself once again at the bottom of the heap, he found that the Lord was there with him again in the mess and muck of prison life (Gen. 39:21). God did not rend the heavens and come down to explain to Joseph how this painful episode fitted into the divine master plan. It did, of course. If Joseph hadn't been falsely accused by Potiphar's wife, he wouldn't have ended up in prison. If he wasn't in prison, he would never have met Pharaoh's servants. If he hadn't met Pharaoh's servants, he would never have been able to save Egypt and his own family when the time of famine came. Much later, Joseph could have looked back and traced the intricate pattern of what God was accomplishing through his suffering. Yet at the time, Joseph was left in prison with no answers to his questions. There in prison, however, in the depths of a situation that must otherwise have cast him into complete despair, the Lord was with him, blessing and prospering everything he did, and blessing others around him as well. There was no answer to his questions about the course of his life, except "I am with you." That is what God had promised Abraham, Isaac, and Jacob, and that is what Joseph experienced: God's faithful presence was with him in the dungeon, every bit as much as in his moments of great success and triumph.

There is one more thing that we need to observe about Joseph's experience: the sign of God being with you is not your success, not even in resisting temptation. The danger of this chapter is that we all want to emulate Joseph's success in resisting temptation, though perhaps without having to suffer similar consequences. We too want to be able to say no to sin in the most trying of circumstances, under the pressure of repeated, insistent temptation. Of course, Joseph's self-control is all the more striking when we remember Judah's lack of self-control under much less extreme provocation in the previous chapter. Tamar did not have to fling herself repeatedly across Judah's path and command him to sin. All she had to do was dress like a prostitute, sit in the right spot, and the rest would follow (Gen. 38:14–18). As we read this chapter, we want to know how we can be like Joseph, who was able to resist such remarkable temptation, when in our daily lives we often find ourselves much more easily led astray like Judah.

What we miss in the process is the fact that God was not at work in Joseph's life because he obeyed God and resisted temptation, and absent from Judah's life because he gave in to temptation and fell into sin. We tend to think that God surely must have loved Joseph because he was such a hero, and must have been really disappointed in Judah because he was such a loser. We then transfer that thought to our own experience: God really loves us when we obey and resist temptation, and hates us, or at least is disappointed in us, when we sin. It is certainly true that God hates sin. But if there is one lesson that is central to the Joseph story, it is that God uses things that he hates to accomplish goals that he loves. He is not just at work in and through Joseph, but in and through Judah as well. Ultimately, the Messiah will come through the line of Judah.

The Lord knew exactly what would happen when he sovereignly brought both Judah and Joseph into temptation. He knew that by his grace, Joseph would remember him and stand, and that Judah would forget him and fall, and that he would use both of these events to accomplish his holy purposes. Joseph would stand as a living, breathing example of 1 Corinthians 10:13: "No temptation has overtaken you that is not common to man. God is faithful, and he will not let you be tempted beyond your ability, but with the temptation he will also provide the way of escape, that you may be able to endure it." Meanwhile, Judah would stand as a living, breathing example of 2 Corinthians 12:9—"My grace is sufficient for you." Yes, someone who sins and falls so spectacularly can still be incorporated into the people and plan of God. In the same way, God will use your sin to humble you and make you appreciate his grace in a way that you never could if he always enabled you to stand strong in the face of fierce temptation.

GRACE AND MERCY

It is that experience of grace and mercy which most increases our love for the Lord and his glory. We can certainly learn from the struggles and successes of others, but our own trials and failed temptations often have the effect of causing us to lean on the Lord far more intensely than we ever learn to do during the good times. We want to live victorious Christian lives in the midst of difficulty, as Joseph did, but many times the Lord's wonderful plan for us is to show us the messy reality that we desperately need God's amazing grace. We don't need God just as our copilot—as someone who assists us to reach our full potential. We need God as our Savior, the one who provides for guilty sinners a free gift of righteousness that we could never attain.

What was God doing in Joseph's life? His dreams were never simply about personal success and preeminence in his family. They were about Joseph becoming a signpost to the gospel, a means by which God's promise to Abraham would ultimately become a reality. The Lord was with him, enabling him to be a blessing to Egyptians in the midst of undeserved pain, betrayal, suffering, and temptation, not simply so that he could become an example for us to imitate (though he is that), but so that he could be an exemplar pointing forward to Jesus. Jesus was the only truly righteous man, the only one who has ever suffered entirely without fault of his own. He experienced far greater temptation than Joseph ever faced. The Spirit led Jesus out into the wilderness to face the full force of Satan's assault, and Jesus did so perfectly (Matt. 4). Joseph may have resisted temptation in this situation, but he was not sinless. There were doubtless times when Joseph lost hope and gave in to self-pity or anger. There were likely times when Joseph did not say, "You meant it for evil, but God meant it for good." Yet in his moments of shining faithfulness, Joseph points us beyond himself to Jesus. The purpose of this passage is not to get you to ask yourself in times of temptation, "What would Joseph do?" Its purpose is to encourage you to ponder what Jesus has done in your place.

Jesus came willingly into the bondage and suffering of this world to serve and bless humanity. The Father was with him, and his presence was a blessing to those around him. He made blind eyes to see and deaf ears to hear, and he proclaimed the good news of God's reign (Luke 4:18). He faced the powerful temptation to choose his own way in the world, bypassing the cross, instead of humbly submitting to God's wonderful plan for his life. Yet he rejected that offer, saying to Satan, "You shall worship the Lord your God and him only shall you serve" (Matt. 4:10). He did so with the full knowledge that the Lord's wonderful plan for his life would take him into the deep darkness of the cross. Where was God on the day when Jesus suffered on the cross? The answer is that we—sinful humanity—meant it for evil. We wanted to do away with the sinless one, whose only crime was to be what humans were intended to be from the beginning. Yet God meant our sin for good, as part of his wonderful and holy plan of redemption. The Father allowed the Son to be falsely accused and falsely condemned, sinfully abused and murdered. Indeed, at the cross, the Father himself treated the Son like a guilty outcast who was stained with the darkest forms of sin. The one who had never done anything other than love and serve God was condemned to experience the agonies of hell, alone in the darkness, forsaken by his own Father.

In that terrible moment, the Father was not with Jesus, so that he might be with us forever. Jesus was bearing our curse there. As a result, the penalty for all those times when we have joined Judah in plunging headlong into sin, instead of siding with faithful Joseph, was paid in full. In its place, we have now been credited with the perfect righteousness of Christ, who withstood every temptation in our place. By his wounds, we are healed. By his righteousness, our filth is dealt with, fully and finally, so that the Lord's smile rests upon us forever for his sake.

This truth gives us assurance and hope as we face the darkest hours of God's plan for our own lives. We will likely have to suffer in this life, and as we do, we may be tempted to believe that it means God is angry with us or has abandoned us. Nothing could be further from the truth. God has poured out all of his anger against our sin on Jesus, which means that our present sufferings can only have a redemptive purpose, teaching us to die to sin and bringing others to see and know the God whom we have met in Jesus Christ. As God enables us, this truth will also help us to say in the face of temptation, "How then could I do such a wicked thing and sin against God?" Even when we fail to do so, and give in again to sin under much less provocation than Joseph, this gospel then reminds us to run afresh to Jesus, the great Shepherd of all wandering sheep, there to find fresh stores of mercy and grace. God loves us more deeply and more profoundly than we could ever have imagined. He is with us and will never leave us nor forsake us. He has wonderful plans to be with you in your successes and in your failures, in your joys and in your trials, sanctifying to you even your deepest distress. Therefore, whatever trials and temptations befall you, you may be sure that the sovereign Lord means it wonderfully for your good and his glory.

FOR FURTHER REFLECTION

1. How did Joseph's situation continue to get steadily worse? How did Joseph respond to trial and temptation?
2. When you face trials and temptations, do you place your hope in changes of circumstances or the promise of God's good purposes?
3. In the face of temptation, when have you failed to do the right thing? When have you suffered for doing the right thing?
4. Have you ever been angry or disappointed with God for not rewarding your faithfulness? What does this reveal about your motivations for obedience?

CHAPTER FIVE

WHEN HOPE GETS PUT ON HOLD (GENESIS 40)

Joseph's story is remarkable and unique. Probably none of us have been sold into slavery by our siblings, or falsely accused of attempted rape and sent to prison on trumped-up charges. Many of us, however, have had experiences of being betrayed and let down by family or coworkers in painful ways. This world is full of difficult and deeply disappointing experiences, and few of us escape unwounded by them. As a result, we can easily identify with Joseph in his sufferings and find hope in God's presence with him in the midst of those sufferings.

Yet Genesis 40 is not about some new suffering that God asks Joseph to undergo. It is about the same old suffering that continues on, long after we think it should be over. This too is something to which we can all relate. We all know what it is to want something good, or to desire relief from something painful, and to desire that change with great intensity. We know how hard it is when that good goal seems to be almost within your grasp, only to have your hopes dashed at the last moment. We know what it is to wait for the phone call that will confirm that you have landed the job of your dreams, or that the relationship you so desire will move forward. But the phone call never comes. Whatever the reason for the lack of communication, the hopes that a few days before were so bright are now gradually fading away. Perhaps there was not a definitive moment that exploded your expectation of a different future—just a slow and gradual deflation of your hopes over days, months, and even years, until you found yourself empty.

THE TURNING POINT WHERE NOTHING CHANGES

That is where Joseph finds himself in Genesis 40. In some ways, this chapter represents the dramatic turning point of Joseph's story. Events are being set in motion that will ultimately result in him being released from prison, elevated to Pharaoh's side, and given power over all of Egypt. Yet Joseph ends this chapter in exactly the same place where he began it, toiling away in prison, seemingly with no prospect of ever emerging from there. What is God up to when he makes us wait and wait for his deliverance? Why would a loving, sovereign God leave us stuck in a situation of painful suffering, when he could so easily and swiftly solve all our problems for us?

First, notice the wonderful irony that dreams were the means that God used to get Joseph out of his pit, since dreams got him there in the first place. Even more than they resented Joseph's fancy coat, his brothers despised his pair of dreams depicting his elevation over them and the entire family (Gen. 37:5–11). When the brothers saw Joseph coming toward them from afar, it was his dreams that were uppermost in their minds. They said to one another, "Let's throw him in a pit and see what becomes of this master of dreams!" (see 37:20).

Now this chapter introduces another pair of dreams, the dreams of Pharaoh's chief cupbearer and chief baker. These men were not lowly servants, but rather would have enjoyed tremendous influence because of their personal access to Pharaoh. However, they had offended him—literally, the text says they had sinned against their master (Gen. 40:1). That's ironic too. These men were in prison because of their real sin against their master, while Joseph, who had refused to sin against God and his master (39:9), was in prison for his righteousness. Since the cupbearer and the baker were the most important prisoners, the captain of the guard assigned Joseph to serve them.

CARING AND BELIEVING

One day when Joseph arrived for work, he saw that his charges were troubled, and he asked them why their faces were downcast. This simple question shows us Joseph meeting and overcoming the first temptation that faces us when our hopes are deferred and our suffering grows long, which is to stop caring about others. These men were Egyptians, and Joseph had no reason to be bonded to them. What did they have to worry about, compared to what Joseph had gone through? He could easily have left them to their worries and gone about his business. Isn't that what we so often do in the midst of suffering? Suffering turns us in on ourselves; our own fears and worries become all-consuming, leaving us with little time or energy to think about others. We desire and expect others to inquire about our sorrows, but the last thing that we want is the burden of someone else's troubles. We have enough of our own already. Yet Joseph saw these men as human beings and cared enough about their concerns to ask them what was going on.

When Joseph asked the reason for their sad faces, the cupbearer and the baker told him that they had had dreams and that there was no professional fortune-teller there to interpret them. The interpretation of dreams was big business in ancient Egypt. After all, a dream might depict a disaster that was about to befall you; if you understood the dream, you could take steps to prepare for your fate or perhaps even forestall it. Joseph's reply to the two men was simple, however. They didn't need a professionally trained interpreter of dreams to explain the future; interpreting dreams was God's business, because he was the one who held the future in his hands. Joseph therefore invited the men to tell him their dreams, so that he might interpret them.

Here we see Joseph facing and overcoming the second temptation that faces us when our suffering grows long: the temptation to lose faith in God. It is easy to see why this happens. If God is not answering our prayers, why would we expect him to answer other people's prayers? You might expect dream interpretation to be a touchy subject for Joseph, given his own experience. Yet in spite of personal disappointments, Joseph still had remarkable faith in God's power and his goodness. He confidently believed that God had given the dreams to these men out of his goodness to communicate with them, and that God was powerful enough to accomplish the things prophesied by the dreams.

Again, don't we struggle with this when our sufferings grow long? We find it hard to keep on believing and hoping that God will really answer our prayers or the prayers of others at this point. Perhaps God isn't really good enough to care deeply about us. Or perhaps we aren't good enough to deserve his intervention. Or perhaps he isn't powerful enough to do what we have asked of him. Gradually our faith and hope ebb away to the point where we no longer ask anything of God or expect anything from him. We feel neglected and abandoned by God, cast onto the trash heap of life.

PERSISTING IN FAITH AND HOPE

If anyone had reason to feel neglected and abandoned by God, surely it was Joseph. He had been sold by his own brothers, falsely accused and thrown into prison for a crime that he not only did not commit, but manfully resisted under great temptation. What prospect was there of Joseph's own dreams being fulfilled? What earthly hope was there of his brothers and parents coming and bowing down to him, the Egyptian prisoner? Yet these experiences did not make Joseph selfishly introverted or bitterly cynical. On the contrary, although there seemed to be no earthly hope of his own dreams being fulfilled, Joseph still believed in a God who does astonishing things and fulfills his promises. He still trusted in God's ability to work through him and held on to his faith that God was up to something important in his life.

What is the explanation for Joseph's faith, hope, and persistent love under such challenging circumstances? The only explanation is the awareness of God's blessing upon him and presence with him, even in the midst of trials. That blessing left him looking for opportunities to serve those around him and direct them to God. For Joseph, the simple words "God was with him" were a game-changing reality in his life. His faith, hope, and love in the midst of such enduring suffering revealed something profound about his heart.

In the same way, our response to ongoing suffering reveals something about our hearts. When our hopes have been disappointed, we may tend to withdraw into ourselves. We retreat into our shells in self-pity, struggling to hold on to our faith and hope in God. At least, I know that I do. When my expectations of life are disappointed, I become "frustrated" (a word I use to conceal the fact that I'm actually angry), and I replay in my head all of the ways in which people around me need to serve and love me. If they fail to do so, I start to resent them. In addition, I begin to resent God for putting me in such a difficult situation and keeping me there. The last thing I am likely to do is to ask what God is up to in this frustrating situation, and how I can perhaps be enabled to serve and love others more effectively because of the painful circumstances in which I find myself.

That response reveals my heart, just as Joseph's revealed his. It is a profound statement of what I believe about God and the world. It shows that at a deep level, I believe that the world exists to fulfill my dreams and aspirations. God himself exists to glorify and enjoy me by making my fondest hopes come true. That is why I feel so let down and betrayed, and why I typically respond by withdrawing from life. I feel that God owes me better than this, or at least owes me an explanation of why my life has to be this way. In the process, I often miss the most precious reality in my suffering, which is God's enduring presence with me.

THE DREAMS

So the two men recounted their dreams. In the cup-bearer's dream, a vine budded, blossomed, and bore fruit all at once (Gen. 40:10). It was as if, under God's bless-ing, the normal agricultural cycle had been dramatically accelerated. The cupbearer took the grapes and squeezed them into Pharaoh's cup, producing instant wine, which he then gave to Pharaoh (40:11). Joseph explained the dream as follows: the three branches represented three days, after which Pharaoh would lift up the cupbearer's head (40:13). "To lift up someone's head" is an idiom from the world of the ancient court. When the king made a public appearance, everyone prostrated himself and bowed his head before him as a mark of respect; how-ever, the king might single someone out and invite him to lift up his head and approach him. This expression can also indicate a royal pardon that means release from prison (2 Kings 25:27).[1] So Pharaoh would summon the cupbearer from prison into his presence and restore him to his exalted position.

[handwritten margin note: Eucharist language – cup, bread (Baker)]

Emboldened by this favorable interpretation, the baker too related his dream, making it sound as much like the other dream as he could. However, instead of his dream depicting his return to his old task under God's blessing, it presented a classic sign of covenant curse, an assault by wild animals (see Deut. 28:26). Unfolding like a Hitchcock movie, the baker dreamed that he was walking along with three baskets of baked goods on his head, powerless to defend Pharaoh's favorite cupcakes from marauding birds. Joseph's interpretation of his dream began exactly like that of the cupbearer: the three baskets represented three days, after which Pharaoh would lift up the baker's head (Gen. 40:19). Yet the baker must surely have suspected that the final outcome would be very different. Whereas the cupbearer would have his head lifted up in the sense of being restored to his previous position, the baker's head would be lifted up in the sense of being hung, with his dead body being left exposed on a tree—the ultimate horror for Egyptians, who obsessed over the proper care of dead bodies.

REMEMBER ME

After Joseph predicted the cupbearer's release, he said to him, "When all goes well with you, remember me and show me kindness" (Gen. 40:14 NIV). More literally, he said, "When it goes well with you, remember me and show me covenant faithfulness (*hesed*), so that I may be delivered from this pit." *Hesed* is a theologically rich concept that combines the notions of loyalty and love. Normally *hesed* describes something that happens within an existing relationship, whether between two human beings or between God and man. In human relationships, *hesed* implies loving your neighbor, not merely in terms of warm emotional feelings, but through acts of love and service that are owed to the other person simply because he is part of the covenant community. God's people are to do justice, to love *hesed*, and to walk humbly with their God (Mic. 6:8). Similarly, *hesed* can describe loyalty to one's obligations to God. This includes faithful actions toward other members of the covenant community, for how can we say that we love our covenant overlord if we ignore his commands to love our fellow vassals (1 John 4:20)?

Yet the most precious use of the word *hesed* in the Old Testament is as a description of what God does. Having entered a covenant relationship with his people, God bound himself to act toward them in certain ways, and he is utterly faithful to his commitment. Psalm 136 explores what the Lord's *hesed* means in its broadest possible terms, for each line concludes with the words, "His *hesed* endures forever." Even when his people sin against him and face the consequences of their sin, they may still appeal to the Lord's *hesed*, as the writer of Lamentations does in the midst of the destruction of Jerusalem in 586 BC. Surrounded by the evidence of the Lord's faithfulness to judge wickedness, rebellion, and sin, he cast himself on the unchanging character of God, affirming, "The steadfast love [*hesed*] of the LORD never ceases; his mercies never come to an end; they are new every morning; great is your faithfulness" (Lam. 3:22–23).

As he appeals to the cupbearer to show him *hesed*, Joseph exhibits remarkable confidence in the faithful fulfillment of the prediction he received from God, given the apparent failure of his own earlier dreams. Put yourself in his sandals for a moment: what must Joseph have felt during the days immediately after the cupbearer was released? At first, he must have welcomed every footstep in the corridor, thinking, "This is it. At last, someone has come to release me from this pit!" It is not coincidental that in verse 15 Joseph refers to the prison as "the pit," using the same word that was used of his place of confinement in chapter 37. After his brothers seized him, his whole life was a succession of pits, from which he so often hoped to be delivered. Now he must have been dizzy with joy at the prospect of the Lord having so providentially provided the means of his release.

But then there must have been the slow, dawning realization that the cupbearer had completely forgotten Joseph; there would be no *hesed* for him, no faithful remembrance. His hopes had been cruelly raised, only to be once more painfully dashed—not just by the cupbearer, but by God himself. It was not just the cupbearer who seemed to have failed to show covenant faithfulness to Joseph; it was the Lord as well. He could easily have brought Joseph's plight back to the cupbearer's remembrance. In spite of Joseph's faith, hope, and love, he still had longer to spend in the furnace of affliction. Surely Joseph must have cried out, "How much longer, O Lord? Haven't I endured enough? Will you forget me forever?"

GOD'S PERFECT TIMING AND ENDURING HESED

God's timing is absolutely perfect, of course, as it always is. If the cupbearer had remembered Joseph sooner, he would have remembered him too soon. Joseph would have been immediately released from prison and lost from sight when God's moment for him came. God's purpose—which at this stage was completely invisible and mysterious to Joseph—was to have him bear witness for him before kings and to deliver both Egypt and his own family from the impending famine. Yet in order for that plan to progress, Joseph had to continue to experience injustice at the hands of men. He had to go on suffering undeserved pain, in order ultimately to free others from death. Time may have accelerated in the cupbearer's dream, but it must have slowed down to a crawl for Joseph as he endured his prison nightmare for two more years until God's time was finally ripe. Nonetheless, God would ultimately work for good everything that Joseph had to endure as evil.

Maybe that is where you are right now. You have been waiting, hoping, praying, and enduring for a long time. You are tired of waiting for God to bring to fruition his plans and purposes in your life. You feel that God has placed you in a pit and forgotten you. Perhaps you too have had to endure the pain of a series of false dawns—moments when it seemed your hopes would finally come true and God would deliver you, only to have those hopes dashed again. Perhaps you too need to be reminded that God's timing is always perfect. There are no accidents with God. You may not understand why you still need to be in the pit. It may make no sense to you right now. Yet what counts is the fact that it makes sense to God, whose wisdom, love, and care are infinitely higher and more profound than yours.

God's wise and loving plans to bring you into extended periods of suffering are not only good for other people, but also good for you. In Romans 5:3–5, Paul says this:

> We rejoice in our sufferings, knowing that suffering produces endurance, and endurance produces character, and character produces hope, and hope does not put us to shame, because God's love has been poured into our hearts through the Holy Spirit who has been given to us.

Paul was no stranger to suffering and, as a result, he also knew the harvest of good fruit that suffering could bring. For Paul, suffering not only doesn't extinguish hope, but actually produces hope by training us in endurance. You cannot learn how to run a marathon by reading a book; the only way to learn how to run the full distance is by long months of training, in which you endure painful stress, gradually building up to greater and greater levels of discomfort. You can't get character from a book either. Character comes precisely from enduring those difficult times, walking with God—and perhaps sometimes trying to run away from God, only to discover that he can run after you faster than you can run away. The one who has promised to be with you forever will not let you go. As Psalm 23:6 reminds us, the Lord's goodness and *hesed* will hunt us down (the word usually translated "pursue" has military overtones) all the days of our lives. The character that comes from enduring suffering produces hope, because we begin to develop enough understanding of our past and present painful experiences to believe that God's faithfulness will take us through whatever suffering our future holds. God never forgets his people or fails to show us *hesed*, steadfast love. He is the Good Shepherd, who has promised that he will hold us safely in his hand. He will never leave us nor forsake us.

Where can you find assurance of God's love and care as you struggle to endure today's trials? How can you know that God's arms of love really are extended toward you, and that he has not in fact forgotten you, especially when he seems to be leaving you in the same pit, year after year? Paul tells us in Romans 5:5 that it is the work of the Holy Spirit to do this. If we cry out to Jesus, using the words of the thief on the cross, "Jesus, remember me" (Luke 23:42), the Holy Spirit takes those cries and presents them before the throne of grace. When we feel like orphans, the Spirit himself bears witness with our spirits that we are indeed the children of God, and if children, then heirs—heirs of God and fellow heirs with Christ, provided we suffer with him in order that we may also be glorified with him (Rom. 8:16–17). This assurance enables us to say with Paul, "The sufferings of this present time are not worth comparing with the glory that is to be revealed to us" (Rom. 8:18).

We cannot do anything to merit such remembrance. We deserve to share the fate of the baker, not the cupbearer. We have truly sinned against our Master, and the wages of such sin is death. And yet, in the ultimate twist of providence, the one to whom we appeal for such remembrance was not merely sold, abused, and wrongly imprisoned; his body was hung upon a tree, under a curse, even though he had committed no crime. Why should my Lord be so cruelly treated, when he exhibited such perfect love toward those around him and enduring faith and hope in God? Why did he have to endure such utterly undeserved sufferings? It was my sin that nailed him there; it was my debt that had to be paid. All of the times when I withdrew resentfully into myself and ignored the needs of others had to be atoned. All of the times when I reviled God's goodness and power and wallowed in unbelief and self-pity had to be judged. The one to whom we cry out, "Remember me!" is the very one we ourselves pierced. Yet this Jesus not only promises to remember us and lift up our heads when he comes in his kingdom, but also to be with us every step of our earthly pilgrimage until we receive our glorious inheritance. What astonishing grace that is!

But not only do we ask Jesus to remember us; he also asks us to remember him. At the institution of the Lord's Supper, Jesus said, "Do this in remembrance of me" (1 Cor. 11:24–25). Jesus tells us to do this, because he knows that it is precisely as we remember him, and especially as we remember his suffering and his glory ("remembering his death until he comes"), that we find help to wait in hope with full assurance of his love and care for us. Suffering—even ongoing suffering—doesn't automatically produce endurance, character, and hope. There are plenty of people who suffer and are soured by it, becoming bitter and cynical. But as the Holy Spirit works in our hearts, reminding us of the amazing love of God that has been given to us in Christ, the same experience that would otherwise make us sour and bitter gradually makes us sweet and tender instead. We slowly become more compassionate toward others in their weakness, joyful in the midst of our pain and disappointment, and filled with hope that God's good purposes will bear gracious fruit in and through us. God ultimately enabled Joseph to recognize that the sins that other people committed against him were under God's sovereign control and would work for his good, as well as for God's divine purpose. May the Spirit instill that confidence in God's sovereign love and gracious faithfulness in each of our hearts too.

FOR FURTHER REFLECTION

1. How did Joseph respond to prolonged suffering?
2. Later God will rescue Joseph from his difficult circumstances. Does God's steadfast love for his people mean that he will always change their circumstances?
3. How does the death of Jesus confirm God's steadfast love for his people?
4. Read Romans 5:3–5. How does the gospel make it possible for suffering to produce hope, rather than hopelessness?

CHAPTER SIX

BECOMING FRUITFUL IN THE LAND OF YOUR AFFLICTION (GENESIS 41)

What a difference a day makes! For Joseph, this day must have dawned like any other. He dressed in the same prison clothing and began to perform the same prison duties as always. Two years had passed since the cupbearer had been released, and Joseph's hopes that he might be remembered had long since evaporated. Then, in the midst of his duties, there was an urgent summons: "Run! Shave! Change your clothes! Pharaoh has summoned you into his presence!" Joseph's period in the pit ended even more dramatically and suddenly than it had begun. He went from the pit to the peak, from prison cell to Pharaoh's right hand, in the course of a single day. How do you cope with such a rapid change in your fortunes? You might think that it would be easy. Yet affluence and prosperity have their own temptations and challenges. Painful memories may continue to dog you. Even when the present seems good, the past still casts its long shadow over you. Every life has its own struggles.

In chapter 41 of Genesis, we see Joseph exhibiting the same qualities in prosperity that he learned during his long period of painful endurance in the pit. In the names that he gave to his sons, we also see him wrestling with the demons of his past. Joseph thought hard about the question, "What is God up to in the pits and peaks of my life?" His answers will challenge all of us to think more clearly about the meaning of our own sufferings in this dysfunctional and dangerous world.

A DRAMATIC TRANSFORMATION

After two years, Pharaoh dreamed two dreams (for all of the dreams in the Joseph story come in pairs). In his dreams, he found himself standing beside the Nile, the source of Egypt's prosperity. Every year, whether it rained in Egypt or not, the Nile would overflow its banks, depositing rich silt, watering the crops, and providing good grazing. It was therefore no surprise that the seven cows that Pharaoh saw coming up out of the Nile were fat. But then seven other cows came up from the Nile behind them; these were thin and evil-looking beasts, and they promptly ate up the seven fat cows without gaining any weight themselves. Then Pharaoh awoke, no doubt in a cold sweat.

After that, Pharaoh fell asleep and dreamed again. This time it was seven fat ears of grain growing on a single stalk, a symbol of astonishing prosperity! But then seven thin ears, wilted by the dry and scorching east wind off the desert, sprang up behind them and swallowed them up. It's no wonder Pharaoh was troubled when he awoke, yet not one of his diviners or wise men was able to interpret his dreams convincingly for him. Pharaoh found himself in exactly the same predicament that the cupbearer and the butler had faced in prison: there was no one to interpret his dreams (Gen. 41:8; cf. 40:8).

Finally, this was the cupbearer's cue to remember Joseph. Faced with the same need, the cupbearer remembered how Joseph had interpreted his own dream. Hence Joseph's sudden summons from the pit. After Joseph had waited patiently to be remembered for two years, now Pharaoh's servants hurried to shave and dress him, making him presentable to the king. Alongside the obvious reversal of fortunes, there is a more subtle reversal here. Each of Joseph's previous misfortunes involved him being stripped of his clothes: his brothers took his fancy coat, and Potiphar's wife grabbed his outer garment. Here his restoration began with the transformation of his clothing.

CONFIDENCE IN GOD

When Joseph appeared before Pharaoh, Pharaoh's greeting was, "I have heard it said of you that when you hear a dream you can interpret it" (Gen. 41:15). Joseph might have been tempted to play along with this flattering invitation to be the indispensable hero. Instead, he immediately corrected Pharaoh: "It is not in me to interpret dreams. But God can, and he will give Pharaoh a response that will set his troubled mind at rest" (see 41:16). Joseph was confident in God and humbly dependent upon him. He did not need to promote himself, even after so many disappointments, because his trust remained in God to protect him and provide for him.

What then does our own boastfulness reveal about our hearts? It shows that we don't really trust God to protect and provide for us, and we don't really regard him as the one we are called to please. Speaking for myself, why do I always feel the need to make sure that people know about my accomplishments? It is because at a deep level I am performing for people. Since people are my audience, the ones I am trusting to satisfy my physical and emotional wants, I need to make sure that they appreciate me and recognize my value. At the same time, that is why I get angry if my family is not properly appreciative of my hard work and diligent efforts. They ought to see and be thankful for how hard I am working for them. Maybe you feel the same way. That would explain why you are so consumed with frustration when your employer doesn't appreciate your work, or your husband and kids don't thank you as they should. This may be why you always need to be the center of attention. But if I remember that God is my audience and that he is the one for whom I am living, then I will be free to give him the credit that he deserves. I will be content to live in his shadow, instead of always pursuing the limelight for myself.

So Pharaoh recounted his dream, and Joseph interpreted it: the dream foreshadowed seven years of prosperity, followed by seven years of grinding famine. Giving that interpretation took some boldness on Joseph's part, because in Egyptian thinking Pharaoh was himself the embodiment of a god. Supposedly Pharaoh's divine power balanced the natural forces and ensured peace and prosperity for Egypt. Yet throughout this encounter, Joseph not only exposed Pharaoh's inability to control the future and provide for his people, but also repeatedly pointed him to God as the one who truly has this power. It was God who had revealed this to Pharaoh (41:25), and God who had shown him what he was about to do (41:28).

Joseph expressed remarkable faith when he said, "The doubling of Pharaoh's dream means that the thing is fixed by God, and God will shortly bring it about" (41:32). Joseph's own dreams, thirteen years earlier, were also doubled, yet until that very morning, he had been languishing in prison. There seemed little prospect of his dreams ever being realized, let alone soon. God's definition of "shortly" is sometimes very different from what we think it ought to be, but his sovereign, good purpose in our lives is nonetheless certain, and he will bring it about in his own perfect timing.

THE EFFECT OF JOSEPH'S TESTIMONY

Joseph's testimony about God made the people around him start taking God into account as well. His bold solution to what was predicted by Pharaoh's dreams was increased taxation. He advised Pharaoh to appoint a reliable and wise man to oversee the famine relief program, which would take and store 20 percent of the good harvests. Then, when the famine came, the government would have the resources to meet the needs of the people. This approach may or may not represent universal wisdom about how to approach the economic cycle of boom and bust. What Joseph was suggesting would undoubtedly be unpopular and a public relations nightmare from the outset. Yet Pharaoh's response to this audacious plan was immediate: "Can we find a man like this, in whom is the Spirit of God?" (Gen. 41:38). Joseph's faith in God was contagious, having an impact even on Pharaoh.

What is truly remarkable, of course, is that we find such an idea remarkable. We are people of such little faith that we rarely believe that the things we say will make a difference, particularly if we are speaking to hardened unbelievers or telling people something that we think they won't want to hear. This applies both to the opportunities that we have to share our faith and, more broadly, to share biblical wisdom in our wider vocations. We often choose to stay silent about our faith in situations where we ought to speak because we don't expect people to respond positively to our words. We have forgotten God's role in the equation. Pharaoh did not respond to the force of Joseph's intellectual argument or to his impassioned rhetoric. God was sovereignly at work in Pharaoh's heart, confirming the truth of Joseph's words, so he immediately found that Joseph's proposal made perfect sense. Might God not also be working in the hearts and lives of some of the people around you and me, preparing them to hear our words, so that they will actually receive that truth with unexpected joy and gladness? It certainly wouldn't be the first time!

Just as Potiphar had put Joseph over his whole house because he saw that God was with him, so now Pharaoh set Joseph over all of Egypt, with the clothing and adornments that went with his new status. He gave Joseph a new Egyptian name, Zaphenath-paneah, which probably means "God lives and sees"—a further acknowledgment of Joseph's God. He also gave Joseph an Egyptian wife, Asenath, the daughter of Potiphera, the priest of On. Prison clothes were replaced by fine linen and gold chains. The family that Joseph had lost back in Canaan was replaced by a new family in Egypt. The false accusations that had led to his public humiliation were now replaced by proclamations that led to public acclamation. His position of powerlessness in prison was replaced by a role with great power at Pharaoh's right hand. Finally his impossible dream of people coming to kneel before him began to be fulfilled when Pharaoh decreed that someone would go ahead of Joseph everywhere he went, crying out "Abrek!"—an Egyptian word that means something like "Make way!" or "Bow down!" Joseph may have had to wait for a long time, but his own dreams were starting to come true.

Everything transpired exactly as Joseph had said. Under his direction, Egypt stockpiled grain during seven years of bumper harvests. It became "like the sand of the sea" so that it was impossible even to keep proper track of the total amount (Gen. 41:49). Then, during the seven lean years, the Egyptians not only had enough for themselves, but also had some for the nations around them. As envoys from many nations joined the Egyptians in bowing down before Joseph, the stage was set for his brothers to reenter his life.

FORGETFUL AND FRUITFUL

What was going through Joseph's mind during the time of great plenty? Did he ever stop to reflect on what God was up to in his life and wonder about things back home? The text tells us what Joseph was thinking by giving us the names he gave to his two sons born during that time. In Genesis 32, the names that Rachel and Leah gave their sons revealed the thoughts of their hearts during that season of their lives. Here too, the names that Joseph gave his boys and the reasoning behind those names reveal Joseph's thinking. He called his firstborn Manasseh because "God has made me forget all my hardship and all my father's house" (Gen. 41:51), and he named the second Ephraim, "for God has made me fruitful in the land of my affliction" (41:52).

What do these names reveal? First, both names affirm that God was doing something in Joseph's life: God made him forget, and God made him fruitful. Isn't the failure to remember that truth one of our constant problems in life? We are convinced that we are doing things (whether good or bad) and that others are doing things (whether for or against us), but we so often forget the overarching truth that God is the primary actor in our lives, shaping us in particular ways according to his own purposes. Joseph's two children were no more accidental than Pharaoh's two dreams or Joseph's additional two years in prison: they were the means by which God was doing something in his life. So too in our lives today, God is shaping everything, the painful as well as the joyful, to accomplish his providential purposes in us and through us in the lives of others. Joseph understood that, and it was crucial to his peace and his faith in the midst of otherwise crushing circumstances.

Second, don't miss the irony of calling one's son "Forgetful." We can understand why Joseph would want to forget his sufferings, but names and their meanings are remembered. Calling his son Manasseh actually assured the perpetual remembering of his declaration of forgetting! How can you constantly remember that you have forgotten something? I think it gives us a different perspective on what it actually means to "forget" painful memories. Perhaps you are wrestling with the reality of life-shaping events that you simply can't forget. These may be terrible sins that other people have committed against you. Alternatively, your own sins and wrong decisions may haunt you continually like a bad dream. What is more, these painful memories from your past continue to affect the way you respond to events and situations in the present. You view people and relationships around you in the present through the lens of those intensely painful events from your past, and the result is chaos and turmoil in your emotions and in your reactions. Well-meaning friends may tell you simply to put these events behind you and move on. But how do you "get over" such a terrible trauma? How can you forget? You cannot simply wipe out the past from your memory banks by an act of the will, as if reformatting the hard drive of a computer. Neither could Joseph.

What Joseph did by naming his son Manasseh was to reshape the significance of the past by putting it into the context of what God was doing in his life. His son became a permanent testimony to God's power to redeem the past. Of course, Joseph could never completely forget his experience of hardship at the hands of his brothers or in Egypt. However, from then on he would remember it through the lens of God's presence with him in his pain and God's faithfulness in ultimately bringing him through that suffering into prosperity. To use an image from the prophet Joel, the Lord had fulfilled his promise to "restore to you the years that the swarming locust has eaten" (Joel 2:25). In Joseph's personal situation, the thin cows of affliction had been consumed by the fat cows of God's providence.

God gave Joseph the grace to put his past hardships and sufferings into a new, redemptive context. The marks of the wounds remained in his life and could never be forgotten, but those scars had been incorporated beautifully into the intricate pattern of God's grace in his life, and Joseph was determined not to forget that. It is the same for us. You don't simply forget an experience of life-changing suffering. You can't. Those scars will mark you indelibly for the rest of your life. Yet what God does by his grace is to take those ugly wounds and reshape them into a beautiful part of the tapestry of purpose and blessing that he is weaving in your life. He can overwhelm the painful memories of your past with the wonderful memory of his greater faithfulness and grace to you in the midst of all your pain and with the assurance that he will bring glorious good even out of your worst suffering.

How does this reshaping of our painful memories happen? The name that Joseph gives to his second son, Ephraim, is a clue. Joseph explains, "God has made me fruitful in the land of my affliction." God doesn't necessarily promise to deliver us *out of* the land of our affliction, though that is what we want and is usually what we pray for. I'm sure Joseph prayed repeatedly to be taken out of the pit and restored to his family in Canaan. Instead, God's purpose for Joseph to be fruitful took shape precisely *in* the land of affliction, in Egypt, where God used him to be a blessing to those around him, ultimately saving many from famine and death.

In the same way, it is often in the land of our affliction that the Lord makes us fruitful, in ourselves and in the lives of others around us. We typically want God to make us into fine decorative china plates, which sit comfortably in a glass cabinet being admired by everyone. Instead, God makes us into serviceable water pitchers that get chipped and scratched and dented through repeated use. That is how our sufferings produce endurance, character, and hope in us (Rom. 5:3–5). It is also how he makes us useful to others around us, who have their own sufferings and difficulties to endure.

THE TRULY FRUITFUL ONE

Yet Joseph is never just a model from which we may learn in these stories. In his original dreams back in Genesis

37, God gave Joseph a vision in which all creation would come and bow the knee before him. In one sense, his brothers were right in seeing this as expressing a reality far bigger than their little brother could ever fulfill. Joseph was a shadow and forerunner of a greater deliverer to come. Before Joseph could even begin to fulfill that calling as a shadow savior, he had to endure repeated and long-lasting suffering that would leave permanent scars. But after that painful preparation, God used him to be a blessing to the nations. In this chapter, Joseph's ministry is described in terms that point back to the Abrahamic promise: the grain piles up "like the sand of the sea" (Gen. 41:49), a clear allusion to the blessing given to Abraham in Genesis 22:17 and repeated to Jacob in Genesis 32:12. Joseph was fruitful and multiplied in the land of his affliction, and the result was life-giving blessing to the nations, first to Egypt and then to all the earth. All who blessed Joseph and bowed the knee before him were blessed and received life. If they refused to bow before him, they inevitably died of hunger.

In this way, Joseph pointed beyond himself to the true Messiah, who was yet to come. Joseph pointed forward to the Christ, who followed the same pattern of suffering and then exaltation and public acclamation. Jesus was not merely second in line behind the Egyptian Pharaoh. He was, and is, the King of kings and Lord of lords, the one before whom every knee will bow and every tongue confess that he is Lord. Yet this one before whom all nations will bow also learned obedience through what he suffered, and became fruitful precisely through his afflictions, as his suffering on the cross brings us life and health and peace.

It is striking that Jesus' resurrected and glorified body still bears the scars of his suffering: there are still nail prints in his hands and a wound in his side. Why didn't the Father heal those wounds at the resurrection, so that Jesus' restored body could be unscarred? It is because these scars that speak of painful sacrifice are made beautiful by the fruit that they bear for God's redemptive purposes.

Jesus will never forget the cross and his profound sufferings at the hands of his brothers. But neither will he forget
the fruit born of that suffering: a new family of men and
women from every tribe and nation, who now receive
new life at his hands. God made that terrible affliction
bear incredible fruit, and those indelible scars now speak
permanently of indelible grace.

Just as Joseph's exaltation was not just for himself,
so too Jesus' exaltation leads to blessing for all nations, if
they will come and bow the knee before him. He himself
is the true bread of heaven, the one whose broken body is
the source of all life. He invites all those who are hungry
to come to him and eat, and all those who are thirsty to
come to him and drink. Jesus doesn't sell his produce to
the highest bidder: he gives it freely to those who have no
money with which to buy. The salvation that Jesus offers
is not based on you performing a certain number of good
deeds, or vowing to quit all your evil habits. It is given to
you freely, without cost. All you have to do is come to Jesus
as a helpless refugee seeking food. You come with empty
hands and nothing to give, asking Jesus to give you the
perfect righteousness that you need to stand before God.
All who come to him on those terms will be welcomed into
his kingdom and will never be sent away. The Father can
never forget those for whom Christ died.

What is more, when God comes into your life, he makes
you forget your sufferings and makes you fruitful in this
land of afflictions. He enables you to set your pains and
difficulties, past and present, in the context of the glorious
inheritance that he has prepared for all those who love
him and are called according to his purpose. He will use
all of the trials and challenges that he brings into your life
to grow your love, your hope, and your faith. He will also
use them to develop your longing for your true homeland,
the place where all of your tears will finally be wiped away
and forgotten, where all of our hearts will finally be healed,
and where the full harvest of God's redemptive work in our

lives will finally be revealed. This world is not our home. This is the land of our affliction. God can and will make you fruitful here by his grace. But we must never forget that there is another land that God has prepared for his people, a land without affliction and pain, where he waits even now to welcome us forever.

FOR FURTHER REFLECTION

1. How did Joseph's elevation parallel his humbling?
2. Despite suffering and yet unfulfilled dreams, Joseph remained confident in God. Is this true for you? Or do you respond by drawing attention to your unjust suffering and deserved recognition?
3. Based on God's revelation, Joseph boldly proposed a plan to bless the ruler and people of Egypt. Has God provided you with opportunities and wisdom to bless others by making and suggesting plans?
4. Joseph's life of painful preparation prepared him to extend life-giving blessing. How did the life and work of Joseph anticipate the life and work of Jesus? How has painful preparation prepared you to extend blessing to others?
5. How does Christ make us forgetful of our suffering and fruitful in our present lives of affliction?

CHAPTER SEVEN

REUNION OR RECONCILIATION? (GENESIS 42)

Reunions of family, friends, or classmates can be times of incredible joy and celebration. There is a wonderful excitement to comparing how quickly the cousins are growing and remembering good times past—and even a perverse pleasure in seeing whose waistline has expanded most rapidly over the intervening years. At other times, however, renewed interaction with long-estranged family members or friends can be edgy, awkward, and hurtful, because reunions are not the same as reconciliation. We can be together without really being together. This is one reason why major holidays often prompt feelings of anxiety, depression, and despair, rather than delight. Genesis 42 traces the story of a reunion that is on its way to becoming a reconciliation. This turning point in the life of Joseph's family is really just the first portion of a much larger unit that stretches from chapter 42 through chapter 45. Even in this opening act of that greater story, however, we get a profound picture of several facets of reconciliation.

THE FAMILY

In the twenty years after the brothers sold Joseph, things did not become any better at home. Genesis 42 opens with Jacob barking at his sons: "Go get some food, you lazy good-for-nothings!" (see verses 1–2). The men who were so ingenious in ridding themselves of their despised younger brother had no plan to save their families from slowly wasting away from famine.

For his part, Jacob was still playing favorites, keeping Joseph's only full brother, Benjamin, back while the others went to Egypt, because "he feared that harm might happen to him" (42:4). That wonderful, fatherly care for Benjamin communicated to the rest of the brothers that they were expendable. Of course, something else may also have been in the back of Jacob's mind. With two decades to think about the circumstances of Joseph's disappearance, Jacob may have grown more than a little suspicious of the brothers' story about what exactly happened in Dothan.

There cannot be reconciliation unless there is a broken relationship. We all have broken relationships, so we are off to a good start. All of us sin and hurt others, and all of us are sinned against and hurt by others. Jacob's family was overflowing with broken relationships. There is plenty of raw material for the grace of God to transform. Jacob sinned against his sons by favoring Joseph. Joseph sinned against the brothers through his arrogance and tattling. The brothers sinned against Jacob and Joseph by making Joseph disappear. There are no innocent parties in life, because all of us sin against others, and all of us are sinned against. The question is not whether we have broken relationships, but what we do with them.

Some of us handle our broken relationships in the way that Joseph did. Perhaps you are entirely content to keep miles and miles between you and the person from whom you are estranged. Joseph ended up a long way away from home against his will, but even when Joseph was elevated to the vice presidency of Egypt, he did not make any effort to reconnect with his family. Even if Joseph could not have left Egypt himself, he could surely have dispatched a messenger. On the contrary, Joseph named his first son Manasseh, "Forgetful," seeking to forget his past hurts in his father's household. For some of us, that is the extent of our desires: we just wish that we could forget.

We cannot simply forget some of our broken relationships, however. In some cases, like that of Jacob and his mutinous sons, you cannot get away from one another. You are stuck in the same office, the same home, or the same marriage. So you do a delicate dance to maintain as much emotional distance from the other person as possible, while still physically occupying the same space, as the days, months, and years slowly grind on. Your prayers echo the old Meatloaf song: "[I'm] praying for the end of time so I can end my time with you."[1] In either case, whether you are physically distant from the person with whom you are estranged or trapped in the same location, you have long ago lost all hope of a real renewal of the relationship. It seems impossible to imagine, outside your ability to accomplish.

THE MEETING

In many cases, that is an accurate assessment: reconciliation is entirely outside our control. In fact, the second major turning point in our story, the meeting of Joseph and his brothers, comes about almost entirely from forces outside themselves. God sent a famine on Canaan and Egypt, which left the brothers searching for food far abroad (Gen. 41:57). What is more, God sent forewarnings of that famine via Pharaoh's dreams, so that Joseph could interpret them, be promoted to Pharaoh's right hand, and enact a famine survival plan to stockpile grain (41:1–44). So in verse 6, twenty years after their treachery, the brothers came to

Egypt and bowed before Joseph, just as in the dreams that triggered the explosion in the first place. No doubt we should see a touch of God's humor there. Fighting against God's plans never works.

Yet it is also clear that God was arranging this meeting as an opportunity, not only for reunion, but also for reconciliation. You can easily have one without the other. All it takes is to make sure that Aunt Susan and Uncle Edmund stay at opposite ends of the Thanksgiving table. Unlike reunion, however, reconciliation can flow only from heart change in all parties involved. There needs to be forgiveness for where you have been hurt and repentance for where you have hurt someone else. As the meeting unfolds, we begin to see the fruit of those heart changes in both Joseph and his brothers.

JOSEPH'S KINDNESS

First, notice that Joseph did not say to his brothers, "I told you so! God told me I'd be the greatest, and here I am!" After completing God's thirteen-year program in humility, Joseph had truly learned the lesson. Notice also how verse 9 highlights the fact that Joseph *did* remember his dream. But *what* Joseph did with his dream now comes full circle. At seventeen years of age, he had dreamed and boasted. A decade later, in his late twenties, Joseph did not boast, but he did try to turn his favorable interpretation of the cupbearer's dream to his own advantage (Gen. 40:14). Ironically, it was at the very pinnacle of his elevation that Joseph finally made the leap from self-interest to service. After interpreting Pharaoh's dream, he suggested a plan of action to protect the lives of others from the coming famine. Shortly before becoming the second most powerful person in Egypt, Joseph finally learned to think of others before himself. So God brought him full circle for a second chance at those first, fateful dreams. This time, Joseph did not boast; instead, he set in motion a plan of action to protect the lives of his family from the coming famine. After all, the second dream had not yet been fulfilled. In that dream, the sun, the moon, and *eleven* stars bowed before him (37:9). However, neither his parents (the sun and the moon in the dream) nor all eleven brothers were here yet.

Even Joseph's test of his brothers demonstrated incredible mercy. Joseph softened his demand from nine brothers serving as hostages while Benjamin was brought from Canaan to one brother. The larger party returning to Canaan would have been able to carry back significantly more grain to feed their families. In addition to the grain, Joseph gave them additional provisions for the journey and secretly repacked their money in their bags (Gen. 42:25). At this point, there were still over five years left of a seven-year famine. The brothers did not know that, but Joseph was generously providing in secret for the needs of their families.

JOSEPH'S ROUGHNESS

Wasn't Joseph also a little rough with his brothers, however? Verses 9–17 read like the interrogation scene of a crime movie, with Joseph playing the bad cop. Four times Joseph accused them of being spies (42:9, 12, 14, 16). All that was needed to complete the scene was a flickering candlestick hanging from the ceiling of the dank dungeon. In their responses, you can hear the brothers cracking under the pressure. Then in verse 17, Joseph has them tossed into prison. That's pretty rough handling. Was Joseph settling old scores and indulging in a little vengeance? We've seen that Joseph was not perfect. Yet whatever clouded motives may have been at work in Joseph's rough treatment, there was a lot more to it than payback.

Part of the purpose of Joseph's interrogation was to gather information. Where were Jacob and Benjamin? Were they even still alive? Don't miss the irony in their response when they proclaimed desperately, "We are honest men" (Gen. 42:11). If they had known Joseph's true identity, they would have appreciated that that line of argument was not their strongest defense. Soon the brothers were panicking: "We're a family of twelve brothers . . . the youngest one is with our father, and uh . . . the other one is no more. We have no idea what happened to him" (see verse 13). That must have brought a grim smile to Joseph's face. The brother they thought to be no more was standing right in front of them.

Beyond that, verses 7 and 8 really emphasize the knowledge gap between Joseph and his brothers. Joseph recognized them, but treated them as strangers. He recognized them, but they did not recognize him. That is not surprising, of course. When they last saw Joseph, he was seventeen. At this point, he would have been about thirty-seven. Then Joseph would have been sporting an adolescent beard and dressed like his brothers. Now he was clean shaven and wearing Egyptian clothing. However, there was something even more fundamental going on here. "To recognize" and "to treat like a stranger" both translate the same Hebrew verb. This verb is used four times in verses 7 and 8. The great turning point in all of their lives thus far was when the brothers had refused to recognize Joseph as a brother, and instead treated him not only as a stranger but as an enemy.

THE TEST

Joseph's big question at this point was, "Have my brothers really changed?" Breaking into Hebrew and asking them point-blank if they were sorry for what they had done would not have worked. Now that Joseph was the second most important person in Egypt, they would have said anything that was necessary. At this point, that would have been in their best interest, just as their treachery had previously been in their best interest. But what if they faced another situation someday when it was again in their interest to betray and abandon a brother? Would they recognize a brother in need this time? Or, when the pressure is on, would they once again treat their brother as a stranger and an enemy? In the upcoming chapters, Joseph will set up three tests to find out whether the brothers have indeed changed.

Joseph understood the difference between forgiveness and reconciliation. The reason some of us struggle to forgive others is that we fail to understand that forgiveness and reconciliation are not the same thing. Forgiving someone does not mean acting as if nothing happened. To take an extreme example, if your father molested you, you can forgive him. However, that does not mean that it would be wise to trust him. Your own children should certainly not visit their grandpa for the weekend alone. But real reconciliation involves the rebuilding of trust when both parties to a broken relationship approach each other in forgiveness and true repentance.

Joseph may have forgiven his brothers, but could he trust them? The first test was his demand that one of the brothers stay in prison in Egypt while the others fetched Benjamin to prove their honesty (42:18–20). Almost immediately, Joseph's test began to yield evidence of true change in the brothers. They said, "In truth we are guilty concerning our brother, in that we saw the distress of his soul, when he begged us and we did not listen. That is why this distress has come upon us" (42:21).

Notice the parallelism that the brothers recognized. Through their own distress, they finally came to understand the distress that they had inflicted on Joseph. In the past, Joseph had primarily been different from them: he was the favored one, the dreamer, the gifted one. Now, as they faced a similar experience of suffering, they began to see Joseph as a fellow sufferer. Suffering can have a

93

powerfully humanizing effect upon our often self-centered worlds. There are limits to the parallel, of course: Joseph had done nothing worse to merit his suffering than being an obnoxious brat, whereas God was now justly punishing them for their grievous betrayal of their brother.

In light of this, verse 22 is a little jarring. As the brothers' hearts were struck with guilt, Reuben seemed to exempt himself because it had not been his idea to sell Joseph—perhaps to avoid serving as the hostage. Joseph had to leave the room at this point, unable to contain his emotions. Alongside the brothers' first confession of sin, this was probably the first hint to Joseph that Reuben, the firstborn, had originally opposed the plot against him.

Joseph's inability to restrain the outpouring of emotional response may explain both why he and why we do not pursue reconciliation with some people. Many of us do not want to revisit old hurts after trying so hard, like Joseph, to forget them and put them behind us. There is a price to pay in revisiting old experiences: old wounds will be reopened, old aches will throb, and many tears will flow. There is no reconciliation without cost.

Regaining his composure, however, Joseph returned, jailed Simeon as the hostage, and sent the rest of the brothers on their way with abundant grain and provisions. He also secretly restored their silver to them (42:25). That kindness also escalated the test. Imagine the scene at the first stopping point, as the donkeys were being refueled, when one of the brothers found his money in his bag. Now these "honest men" were left looking like they had not paid for their purchases. The rest of the way home to Canaan, they would have been watching the rearview mirror for a chariot with flashing lights.

This heightened the test of the brothers' loyalty. To win back Simeon's freedom, they now needed to return with Benjamin while they knew themselves to be under suspicion of theft. Joseph was creating a test that mirrored their betrayal of him. The brothers had treated Joseph like a stranger, trading his life for silver. Would the brothers now demonstrate repentance and changed hearts, or would they just "take the money and run"?

THE OBSTACLE

After discovering the money in their sacks, the question of what the brothers should do next was put on hold until they arrived back home. When the brothers told Jacob "all that had happened to them" (Gen. 42:29), they glossed over the more alarming details of their rough treatment, the three days in prison, and Simeon's imprisonment. They even ended the story by giving the impression that they were on the verge of negotiating favorable trading terms (42:34). However, that rosy picture unraveled quickly when they started unpacking. They now realized that not just one, but all of the brothers still had their money. Perhaps understandably, Jacob's worst suspicions were confirmed. Here they were, once again a brother short, with an incredible story and flush with cash. Were his sons playing some twisted television reality show in which each week a new brother gets voted off the island and sold into slavery? Jacob's suspicions were no longer cloaked when he accused them in verse 36, "You have bereaved me of my children: Joseph is no more and Simeon is no more." Whatever had happened down in Egypt, Jacob was increasingly confident that he knew who was responsible. Jacob therefore decided to cut his losses, to abandon any hope of recovering Simeon, and to refuse to release Benjamin.

As the chapter closes, we are back in a very familiar place, this time with Jacob as the obstacle to the reconciliation of the family. We are still waiting and wondering. Joseph is waiting and wondering whether the brothers have really changed. Simeon is waiting in prison, wondering if anyone will come to rescue him. The brothers are waiting and wondering if they will ever be able to return for Simeon. Time and again in the story of Joseph, we have encountered the painful reality of hope deferred.

It is perhaps appropriate that we should encounter that painful reality here, as God begins to bring about the reconciliation of this family on his own timetable. The truth is that many of us live, sometimes for many years, with our hopes of reconciliation constantly deferred. There may be many reasons. Some of those reasons may be good, while others may be wrong. Some reasons are wise, while some are foolish. Some factors are within our control, while others are not.

THE GOOD NEWS

We are all deeply flawed people, sinning against and hurting one another. We often long desperately to overcome the shame of our sins against others and the pain of others' sins against us. But at the same time, we often only view the sought-after reconciliation horizontally, looking at other people. When our vision is limited to our interactions with one another, we inevitably end up facing the great chasm of sin—ours and theirs—that lies between us.

However, running through the story of Joseph's family—as well as of the whole Bible and of history—is the even more profound truth of the gospel. The truth is that our situation is both far worse and far better than we could ever have imagined. It is far worse than we think because the things we do to each other are the evidence of our fractured relationship with the One who made us, takes care of us, and sustains our very life. The great turning point in the brothers' self-awareness came when they began to see that the evil they had done against Joseph was first and foremost a sin against God, deserving of punishment. Yet at the same time, our situation is far better than we can imagine because the God against whom we have offended has already reconciled us to himself. If God had been primarily interested simply in paying Joseph's brothers back for their sin, why not leave them in Canaan to die from the famine? That was not God's plan, however. Long before they realized their guilt, God had already put everything in place to save their lives. Most amazing of all, their salvation hinged on God using their worst sin to accomplish his saving purposes. The betrayal of the best-loved son of their father, which led to his enslavement, suffering, humiliation, and unjust imprisonment, became the means by which God raised him to a position of power and influence for the saving of many lives.

Just as a room may be lit, so that through a doorway you see someone's shadow on the wall before they themselves walk through, so Joseph foreshadowed the coming, so many generations later, of his distant nephew, Jesus. Jesus, the beloved Son of his Father, became our brother in order to suffer injustice, humiliation, and death at our hands, for our sin. Jesus then rose from the dead and was exalted to the highest place. From there he gives us new life, the Spirit, and resurrection hope.

Unlike Joseph, Jesus did not wait until prompted by circumstances to pursue reconciliation with us. Jesus, the Father, and the Spirit have known from before all time exactly how they would right our wrongs and undo our evil. On the cross, Jesus bore the penalty for our sin and the shame of our suffering, while the Spirit now applies to us all of the benefits of his unbroken oneness with the Father. So when Jesus calls us to believe in him, it is the call to recognize him both as our brother, like us in every way except sin, and as our Lord, who rules over us for our protection, our good, and our joy. The Spirit gives us that very faith to believe. And when Jesus tests our hearts through the trials and disappointments of life, it is not to discover an answer about us that he does not know, but rather to reveal to us the growing fruit of the new life that he has planted in us.

RECONCILIATION

What does this have to do with all these people with whom I cannot get along? How does it speak to my relationship with that person whom I cannot stand, that I cannot fix, and with whom I cannot renew friendship despite my best efforts? Through Christ, we can access the building blocks of reconciliation: confession of our sin, repentance, and forgiveness of the sins of others. Because my sin has been paid for by Christ, I can confess it freely and not be crushed by it. I do not have to deny my sin or minimize it. Because Christ has given me his heart-changing Spirit, I can begin to repent, turning away from my habitual sins that repeatedly hurt others. Because Christ is the Lord and Judge, I can entrust to him the fitting judgment of those who have sinned against me and hurt me.

Jesus has not only given us the building blocks of reconciliation, but has also given us a place to learn how to use them: the community of believers, the church. The church is rather like preschool in the process of reconciliation. It is not always a smooth and comfortable place to be. One of the building blocks may go sailing across the room. Or one kid may use one to smack another on the head. We can turn even confession, repentance, and forgiveness to self-serving ends. But through the bumps and bruises we acquire along the way, we are learning the skills that we desperately need, so that we might go out into the world to be healers, builders, and renewers.

But, you might say, that's exactly the problem. Some of those people whom I want most to grow toward are fellow believers. It is other Christians with whom I still struggle to rebuild trust, friendship, and fellowship. *Exactly!* All of us are mid-story. All of us, in certain relationships, are living in the hiatus at the end of chapter 42. We are all waiting for the climax and resolution, not only of our own personal stories, but of the great story of God's reconciliation of all things in Christ. We may taste occasional sweet sips of that coming day in this life through the renewal of once-broken relationships. Yet the fullness remains before us as our ultimate hope.

I saw that hope embodied in the sometimes frustrating relationship between my wife and her grandmother. Mama was a lifelong believer, who loved all of her grandchildren. But despite many similarities between them, my wife never seemed to enjoy Mama's approval and never really understood why. Then, a few years ago, Mama passed away. To my surprise, Rebecca's response was one of relief. She was not glad that her grandmother had died; rather, she understood that when she next saw Mama, they would both be in glory, free of their sin, finally able to communicate without misunderstanding, able at last to truly love and enjoy one another. They will not only be reconciled to one another, but will together enjoy unbroken fellowship with Jesus, bowing before him and confessing him as Lord together at the great reunion of God's reconciled family.

FOR FURTHER REFLECTION

1. How does the passage highlight God's activity in the reunion of the brothers?
2. Joseph showed kindness to his brothers before full reconciliation occurred. What kindnesses could you show to family or friends, whether or not you are reconciled?

3. In your relationships, are you willing to bear the cost of reunion, forgiveness, and rebuilding of trust? In what ways do you need to demonstrate a repentant and changed heart?

4. Unlike Joseph, Jesus sought us out, despite our betrayal of the Father, and bore the cost himself for our lack of love toward God and others. How does this work of Jesus free us to extend forgiveness and express repentance?

5. While God does not promise reconciliation in all of our earthly relationships, what other hope does the gospel provide?

CHAPTER EIGHT

MAKING PEACE
(GENESIS 43)

How do you restore a broken relationship and overcome the profound breach that sin causes? Small sins can easily be forgiven. If someone agrees to meet you for dinner at a certain time and is ten minutes late, his offense can easily be overlooked. Major crimes, however, are a different story. People are appropriately outraged when a child abuser receives a trivial sentence that doesn't match his crime. It is the same way in personal relationships. When someone has sinned against you in a traumatic, life-altering way, just saying sorry doesn't seem enough. Forgiving someone who has sinned against us deeply is not necessarily the same thing as being reconciled to them and restored to a new relationship. We cannot just pretend that nothing happened, or that their sin was not serious. To be truly reconciled, there needs to be repentance and remorse over the sin, the kind of genuine repentance that issues in a changed life.

RESTORING SHALOM

That is what God was up to in this part of the story of Joseph. God wasn't merely using Joseph as a convenient pawn to provide the food that Jacob's family needed to survive a major food crisis. His goal was to restore and renew the family's deeply broken relationships, and for that to happen Joseph needed to be able to see that his brothers had changed. The key word in this chapter is *shalom*, "peace," which occurs four times in Hebrew, even though it doesn't always appear as the same word in our English translations. The steward greeted the nervous brothers with words of *shalom* in verse 23 when they entered Joseph's house. Then Joseph himself asked after their *shalom* and the *shalom* of their father in verse 27, and the brothers responded by assuring Joseph of Jacob's *shalom* in verse 28. To see the significance of this theme, you have to remember that the *shalom* of this family was shattered long before Joseph's brothers ever sold him into slavery. In Genesis 37:4, the brothers couldn't even say *shalom* to Joseph because of the bad report he had brought against them. It was in pursuit of *shalom* that Jacob sent Joseph out to visit his brothers on the fateful day of his abduction; Joseph was supposed to inquire about their *shalom* and the *shalom* of the flock (37:14). Now God himself was going to rebuild the family's *shalom*, restoring long-broken relationships to a better-than-new condition. Our God is in the business of making unlikely peace in fractured families.

Of course, this was no ordinary family. In Genesis 35:11, God promised Jacob that his family would become a "company" (*qahal*, church) of nations—a harmonious band of brothers dwelling together in unity. However, between Jacob's toxic favoritism, Joseph's slanderous report, and the brothers' murderous envy and slave-dealing, the promise seemed impossibly broken by human sin. It is little wonder that when Joseph was emancipated and enthroned, he made no effort to contact his father or brothers. He thought that he was finished with that painful chapter of his life. Revealingly, he named his oldest son Manasseh ("Forgetful"). He wanted to turn the page and move on, forgetting his father's household and the sufferings that they had inflicted on him.

Yet God's plans for Joseph and his brothers were different and more gracious. God initiated the next phase of the story by sending a famine that became both the means that raised Joseph to his position of power in Egypt and also the circumstance that required his brothers to travel there for food. It was God who enabled Joseph, upon recognizing his brothers, to resist the temptation to have them immediately imprisoned and executed. God planned another chapter in the story of this family, in which Joseph would finally be reunited to his father and reconciled to his brothers. Their *shalom* would be restored, and God's promise of a united family of faith would be fulfilled.

This is a word of hope to us as well. Perhaps at present there is no *shalom* in your family. People are sinning against each other in little and big ways, and the brokenness is evident to all. You might be tempted to turn the page and move on, trying simply to forget your family and the pain that they have caused you. The *shalom* of your family will not necessarily be healed this side of heaven. God does not deal with every family in the same way, nor does he heal every hurt of our hearts here and now. Yet this story reminds you that God has the power to heal even your family. Sometimes he restores our brokenness in remarkable ways in the present. The end of your story—and the story of your family—is not yet written, so don't give up hope of remarkable reconciliation. Of course, even if your family remains unreconciled here on earth, ultimately God has a plan for the complete *shalom* of all of his people in heaven. There all of our families will finally be made whole, all of the sinful brokenness that now causes us such pain will be fully healed, and all of the tears we have shed over our families will be wiped away as we are made fully one in Christ.

In this chapter, we are going to look more closely at the way in which God healed the *shalom* of each member of this particular family. We will also explore the bigger implications of this restoration for the haunted, strife-ridden world in which we live, a world where there is no lasting *shalom* within the human family or between humanity and the Father God who created us.

JACOB AND HIS BROTHERS

First, let's look at the story from the perspective of Joseph's brothers. When they came down to Egypt the first time, Joseph treated them harshly, accusing them of being spies. He insisted that Simeon remain in Egypt as a hostage until they brought back their youngest brother, Benjamin. At the same time, he secretly treated them generously, returning their money in each of their sacks. Strikingly, it was Joseph's kindness, rather than his harshness, that first drew the brothers to speak fearfully and wonderingly about God, saying, "What is this that God has done to us?" (Gen. 42:28). This is the first time that we hear God's name on the lips of the brothers, and it represents a sign of the change that was already taking place in them. Their guilty consciences were primed for change. Yet Joseph's kindness also (deliberately?) put the brothers in a difficult situation. If they returned to Egypt, would they be treated as thieves who had absconded without paying for their grain? How would they explain to their father once again returning home without one brother, but with an abundance of cash? It looked suspicious to say the least. To lose one brother might be a misfortune, but to lose two smacked of carelessness or worse.

That, of course, was how Jacob saw it, and he was determined not to let Benjamin go down to Egypt, even though it meant giving up any hope of Simeon's return (42:38). There was a stalemate. God's plan was not so easily thwarted, however. The famine became even more severe, forcing Jacob and his sons to revisit the question of a return to Egypt. When Jacob suggested that the brothers go back to Egypt without Benjamin, Judah made it clear that that was not an option. He was willing to pledge his own personal honor and fortune as a surety of his brother's safety, but they could not go down there without Benjamin. Should he fail to bring Benjamin back, he would "bear the blame forever" (43:9). This time, reluctantly, Jacob accepted Judah's offer and released Benjamin into their care.

It is striking that Judah, the same brother who formulated the plan to sell Joseph in Genesis 37, provided the lead in this new mission. The mention of a pledge in verse 9 also connects this story with Genesis 38 and the pledge that Judah offered Tamar in exchange for their brief fling. These similarities invite us to see the differences between the stories as well. In Genesis 37 and 38, Judah's successful plan and the offer of his pledge were both designed to serve himself and advance his own interests, while here they were designed to serve others at whatever cost to himself. God was at work, changing Judah even before he made the trip back to Egypt. It was not yet a complete change, of course. There was no confession here by Judah of the ways in which he and his brothers had sinned against their father in the matter of Joseph. But substantive change is not often a sudden, 180-degree turn. It usually happens in small, incremental steps.

Perhaps that is something you should be looking for in your strained and shattered relationships: small steps toward change. Sometimes we demand unrealistic levels of transformation from people and refuse to make any concessions until the other person has changed completely. But change is a process, and we can often recognize and celebrate baby steps in the right direction, while still acknowledging that the process has a good deal further to go. Sometimes we ourselves are the ones who need to change. We recognize that we are the ones who have sinned and are sinning against those around us, yet we do not have the power to transform ourselves. God's work of sanctification in our hearts is often a slow process, in which it is appropriate to recognize and celebrate every step in the right direction.

THE RETURN TO EGYPT

So the brothers returned once again to visit the mysterious man who ran the whole of Egypt, this time with Benjamin in tow (Gen. 43:15). Their treatment when they arrived was completely unexpected, however. Once again, they were not treated like other people. They were invited to a meal at the house of their unrecognized brother, Joseph (43:16). This unusual invitation caused them considerable concern; they immediately remembered the strange occurrence on the first trip, when they found their money returned to their sacks. They also conjectured that perhaps their host was after their donkeys—a rather far-fetched idea, considering he had all the power and riches of Egypt at his disposal. If he was interested in their animals, he could have been more direct about it.

In fact, Joseph had a more delicate target in mind than their donkeys. He was after their hearts. So the meal to which they were invited unfolded like the climax of a murder mystery in which the detective gathers the suspects together and arranges a reenactment of the crime in order to wring a confession out of the guilty conscience of the murderer. When the brothers expressed their fears about the mysterious return of their money to the steward, he explained it as an act of God—specifically "the God of your father," a remarkably Israelite turn of phrase for an Egyptian (43:23). This speech was presumably scripted by Joseph himself to remind his brothers of the omnipotent power of their God, who was able to work even in faraway Egypt. Meanwhile, Joseph heightened the sense that mysterious forces were at work by arranging the brothers in exact order of age when he drew up his seating plan for the meal. No wonder they looked at one another in astonishment (43:33).

Finally, when the meal was served, Joseph made sure that while they all had plenty to eat, Benjamin received five times as much as his brothers (43:34). It was plain for all to see which of the brothers was the favorite in this apparently divinely ordained scenario. If there was still jealousy and enmity at work among the brothers, this would surely stir it up. On the next day, he would give the brothers a perfect opportunity to dispose of this unloved favorite without any blame attaching to them. They could go home with the food they needed, without the brother that they hated, and with an unimpeachable excuse. In order to give the story about a stolen cup maximum credibility, Joseph arranged for them to drink and make merry (43:34). Elsewhere, this clearly means to get drunk (e.g., Jer. 25:27). He wanted the brothers to have only hazy memories of the night's celebration, to make them believe that it was possible that Benjamin had indeed stolen the cup.

Notice the cost to Joseph of this elaborate scheme to elicit evidence of repentance. Biblical narrators don't often show us the internal emotions of the characters, but here he tells us that Joseph was so overcome by emotion that he had to go to an inner room and weep (43:30), just as he did on their previous visit. Joseph was not orchestrating events stoically from a safe distance; he longed to be reunited with his brothers. However, for real reconciliation to take place, it would be necessary to see whether real change had occurred in his brothers.

That, of course, is true if our own broken relationships are to be restored. It is not only the guilty party who has to pay the price of reconciliation. The person who has been sinned against also has to be willing to bear the cost. There will usually be many tears on both sides of the equation before *shalom* can be restored. Sometimes it might seem easier to forget the whole endeavor and go back to living unreconciled lives; at other times, there may be the temptation to gloss over the sin and rush to reconciliation before real change has taken place. Pursuing true reconciliation is a hard and costly process, demanding much of all those concerned.

JACOB'S FEARS

Meanwhile, what of their father Jacob? He was left sitting at home all alone, waiting for news. In some ways, that was a fitting consequence of his toxic favoritism, which was still on display. Jacob persisted in clinging to Benjamin, even though it meant that Simeon could never return. That evaluation spoke volumes about the relative worth of the sons in their father's eyes. Actually, in all of this, Jacob was concerned primarily for himself. Faced with the loss of Simeon and the potential loss of Benjamin, he said, "You have deprived me of my children. . . . Everything is against me!" (Gen. 42:36 NIV). When he sent the brothers on their way to Egypt, his final cry was filled with angry resignation and self-pity: "If I am bereaved of my children, I am bereaved" (43:14). Never mind the fact that if Jacob was bereaved, then his sons were, by definition, dead. In spite of everything Jacob had gone through, he remained a proud, self-centered old man. From his first failed efforts to steal the birthright in his own strength, through his conflicts with Laban, to his wrestling with God at the fords of the Jabbok, God had pressed home on Jacob the lesson that his attempts to live out of his own resources would never bring him peace. Even now, however, it seems that the message of God's irresistible grace and loving favor sovereignly at work in his life had not yet truly taken hold of Jacob's heart.

The irony is that the fate that Jacob most feared, losing his beloved son, was the very last thing that God had in mind. He did not want to shatter his *shalom*, but to restore it to a new and better state. Rather than mourning the loss of Benjamin, Jacob would receive Joseph back, as if from the dead. First, though, God had to break the toxic grip on Jacob's life that was held by his idolizing of Rachel's children. That idolatry was evident in Jacob's response when Joseph disappeared. He did not simply grieve, but grieved as one who would not be comforted: "No, I shall go down to Sheol to my son, mourning" (Gen. 37:35). When the brothers first suggested taking Benjamin down to Egypt to retrieve Simeon, Jacob's reply was: "My son shall not go down with you, for his brother is dead, and he is the only one left. If harm should happen to him on the journey that you are to make, you would bring down my gray hairs with sorrow to Sheol" (42:38). To Jacob, life without Joseph and Benjamin would become a living Sheol: a hopeless, shadowy existence, without meaning or purpose.

God wanted Jacob to bury the idols of his heart, as he had buried his household's physical idols at Shechem on his return to the Promised Land (Gen. 35:4). To achieve this goal, God had to take from him his beloved Joseph and then Benjamin, in order that he might receive them both back, purified. Jacob had to be left completely alone, bereft of all of his children, so that he would once again be forced to trust in God alone to fulfill the Abrahamic promise that he would have descendants like the sand of the sea. God put Jacob in a situation where he would have to walk by faith in the promise of God over the many months before he would see his sons again. He was old, and their journey was long and perilous. He had nothing to comfort him in that situation except the bare word of God's promise.

What are the idols to which you and I cling so tightly that we cannot imagine life having meaning and value without them? Where do you find yourself saying to God, "Give me this or my life will not be worth living"? Is it a particular relationship? The blessing of having a family? Your need for a job? Your desire for health? Or perhaps it is your longing for a better relationship, or a way out of your dead-end job, or a family that doesn't hurt you in the way that they do. Notice that all of these are good things. There is nothing wrong with wanting good health, or a fulfilling job, or relationships that sing, any more than it was wrong for Jacob to love his sons. It was the excessive desire that was Jacob's problem; he clung to them with a death grip that would not yield to God's greater and more loving wisdom. That's the mark of an idol, and God in his gracious jealousy will not share you with an idol. He wants the whole of your heart. As a result, he will sometimes lovingly pry your fingers away from whatever you hold most dearly, so that he may give it back to you again—purified, enriched, and better than you could ever have imagined.

THE LIMITS OF OUR IMAGINATION

One problem that we share with Jacob is that our imaginations are so limited. Why did Jacob cling to Joseph and Benjamin so tightly? I think it was more than simply an emotional attachment to Rachel, their beloved mother. On some level, Jacob was thinking about the Abrahamic promise, and behind that the Adamic promise, of a Son through whom all the families of the earth would be blessed, who would finally crush the Serpent's head (Gen. 3:15; 12:1–3). It seemed obvious to him that the line of promise would go through his union with his beloved Rachel and thus through Joseph, or, failing that, Benjamin. That is why he honored Joseph with the wonderful coat; that is why he treasured Joseph's dreams; that is why his agony at Joseph's death and at the prospect of Benjamin's loss was so desperate. To Jacob, their death spelled the inevitable end of the line for the Abrahamic promise: no more Messiah.

How little Jacob understood the ways of God! God had sovereignly chosen him ahead of his brother Esau, and the messianic line would not go through Rachel. Instead, God chose unloved Leah to bear Judah, the child from whose line the Messiah would come. Not only would Judah be the father of the promise, but the mother would be Tamar the Canaanite, Judah's own daughter-in-law. In other words, God took one of the greatest sins of Judah's life and turned it into the means of providing the greatest blessing that the world has ever seen. In the same way, God would take the greatest sin of all the brothers and use it as the means of saving all their lives and keeping alive the line of promise. Jacob would not be bereaved forever, as he feared when he said good-bye to Benjamin. God's purpose for him was better than that—far beyond his wildest imaginings. Instead of losing Benjamin forever, he received him back, along with Simeon and Joseph. Jacob could do nothing to protect God's plan, but he didn't need to. God was more than capable of blessing him without his assistance.

To what are you clinging for all you are worth? What are you so fearful of losing, or of never having? Perhaps you justify the strength of your grip on your idol by saying, "This is a good thing! It must surely be God's will for me!" Well, if it is so surely God's will for your life, you can loosen your fingers a bit and trust it all to his grip. God's purpose for you is good beyond your wildest imaginings. In pursuit of that good purpose, he will graciously bring you into painful and challenging situations that expose the idolatries of your heart. His goal in doing so is not to destroy your *shalom* and leave you bereaved, though it may feel that way. Instead, his goal is to free you from your idolatries and give you a new and deeper *shalom* that is rooted in the gospel, by which you have been reconciled to him.

The promised seed, the true descendant of Judah and Tamar, was God's own beloved Son, Jesus Christ. Far from clinging to him fearfully, the Father sent him into this broken and pain-filled world to restore our broken *shalom*. Where we instinctively move away from suffering and flee from pain, God chose to enter our world and embrace the pain and suffering that came with that choice. The Father knew what our reconciliation would cost Jesus and what the cost would be to himself. Jesus was not the only one who wept over Jerusalem, devastated at the hardness of hearts that kept people from coming to him for forgiveness (Luke 19:41). The Father also knew that his own chosen people would reject and scorn him, preferring their darkness to the light that Jesus came to bring (John 3:19). He knew that Jesus' earthly brothers would take him and sell him for silver, before torturing and killing him. What must it have done to the Father's heart to watch his beloved Son undergo such terrible agony?

Yet that painful journey through a world of suffering and brokenness was necessary for Jesus in order to heal our shattered *shalom*, reconciling us to God at the cost of his own blood. God himself paid the full price of our reconciliation to him. All we have to do is bow our hearts before him, acknowledging that we have wandered far away, and asking him to receive us back into his favor. The salvation that we have received in Christ is far greater than anything we could have imagined or dreamed up for ourselves: God himself pays the desperate debt that we owe, in order that we may receive the glorious inheritance that Christ earned. In that reality is a peace that no circumstance in the world can ever shatter or destroy. If God is for us, who can be against us? And if God is for us, then we may now begin to seek the peace of those around us, being reconciled to them in spite of the painful cost to ourselves.

FOR FURTHER REFLECTION

1. What is *shalom*? How was the *shalom* of Joseph's family shattered?
2. How do we normally respond to the broken peace of our families, churches, or communities?

3. Jacob turned the good gifts of God's promise and his son into idols. What good things have you turned into idols?

4. What real change needs to take place in you to move toward restoring *shalom* in your relationships? If that change is large, what are small steps you can take in the right direction?

5. Jesus gave us peace (John 14:27) by leaving the *shalom* of heaven and enduring the forsakenness of broken *shalom* with the Father that we deserved. How does that change our approach to our fractured relationships?

CHAPTER NINE

RECONCILED AT LAST (GENESIS 44:1–45:15)

Many classic books and films explore the way in which unresolved guilt can eat away at a person's soul. Think of Lady Macbeth, endlessly scrubbing her hands to try to remove the scarlet stain of her sin of murdering the old king. Peace is not easy to find in this broken and fallen world, since we are all both sinners and sinned against, victims and victimizers. That means we all constantly have to deal with the bitter effects of other people's sins against us and with our own guilt over our sins against others.

For many of us, this reality is a low-grade background hum in the ambience of our existence. Yet from time to time it breaks into the foreground of our thinking when we commit a public sin or when we are sinned against in a dramatic way. In those seasons of life, the question of how to deal with our own sin and how to respond to the sins of others against us becomes *the* big issue with which we have to deal. The answer in these moments of crisis, however, is no different from the answer that we need to apply to our hearts daily in order to deal with the constant, painful throb of everyday, ordinary, dysfunctional life. We all need a substitute who is willing and able to pay the price of our sin and bear the estrangement that it has brought into our lives, and we need a God who is willing and able to bring profound and glorious good out of the most wretched and terrible experiences of our lives. This passage of Genesis points us to that wonderful good news.

GUILT UNCOVERED

At the end of Genesis 43, we left the brothers on their second trip to Egypt to buy grain, with Joseph getting them so drunk that they would have only hazy memories of the night's events. As they loaded their donkeys and headed back to Canaan, perhaps Simeon was wondering to himself, "Did I really stand on the table and belt out a karaoke version of 'Can You Feel the Love Tonight'?" Maybe Levi was recalling throwing up in one of the potted plants. Overall, however, they must have been feeling intensely pleased with a successful conclusion to a dangerous mission. They had gone down to Egypt safely, they were bringing back abundant food, and for once they had more brothers on the return trip than on the outward journey.

Nothing sobers a person up faster than the sound of sirens and the sight of flashing lights. Before the brothers knew it, they were metaphorically being pulled over on the hard shoulder of the highway and grilled about the whereabouts of their host's missing silver goblet. The brothers were full of aggrieved innocence. "Why would you even think such a thing?" they said. "We brought back the money that we found in the sacks the first time, so why would we steal something else now? If you find the cup, the person who stole it shall die and the rest of us shall be your servants" (see Gen. 44:8–9).

It is interesting to observe what legalists we all are whenever we feel ourselves to be innocent. The brothers demanded the ultimate punishment for the person who had offended like this, breaking the sacred trust of

Eastern hospitality by stealing the host's cup. What, then, should the appropriate penalty be for someone who stole his brother's life and condemned him to a lifetime of servitude? Aren't people more valuable than cups? Yet if that scenario had been presented to the brothers, they would have found reasons why their case was exceptional. We are all ready to condemn people who commit sins that we cannot conceive of committing ourselves. Yet when it comes to our own sins, we are much less eager for swift justice. There are always extenuating circumstances in our case, reasons why we were not fully responsible for our actions, or reasons why mercy should nonetheless be offered to us. When we say harsh words to others, or are critical and rude, we didn't really mean it or we couldn't help ourselves. The excuses and denials quickly flow for ourselves, but when it comes to others, we insist that strict justice must be done.

This is probably one of the reasons why we find reconciliation so hard: we lack the imagination to put ourselves in the shoes of the person who has sinned against us and find it hard to think of ourselves in their situation. We think that we would never sin like that—ignoring all of the parallel ways in which we sin daily. Because we are able to distance ourselves from the other person, it is easy for us to demand from him the pound of flesh that justice requires. If we can see ourselves as fellow sinners, however—people equally capable of sins that justly deserve death, who need compassion and forgiveness as much as anyone else—then it becomes easier for us to show compassion and forgiveness to others when they sin against us.

Unimpressed by the brothers' protestations of innocence (not least because he had himself earlier planted the allegedly stolen cup in Benjamin's sack), the steward began to open their sacks one by one. As with the seating at the banquet, he started with the oldest, Reuben, and worked his way down to Benjamin (Gen. 44:12). As he opened the sacks and the brothers saw that their money had again been returned, they must have had a sinking feeling. Perhaps they felt doomed to be haunted forever by the silver that they had received in exchange for their brother. That sinking feeling must have turned to profound panic when the steward got to Benjamin's sack and the missing goblet was found inside. Of course, they all knew that it had been planted there, just like their money. But what were their chances of convincing a judge of that fact, especially when they were to be tried before the man who seemed to have planned their downfall? Was there not evidently a higher hand at work in all of this—a connection that the steward had been hammering home from the beginning, with his assertion that their God had returned their money to them on the previous trip (43:23)? The logical conclusion was that this time their God had not only returned their money, but also miraculously planted the cup in order to pay them back for their former misdeeds.

That was precisely the conclusion that Judah drew when they appeared before Joseph. He said, "God has found out the guilt of your servants" (Gen. 44:16), referring not to the cup, which only Benjamin could plausibly have been charged with stealing, but to their earlier sin of stealing Joseph. He recognized a kind of cosmic karma at work, in which their secret sin had come back to haunt them. But Judah recognized that this circumstance was not the work of blind fate. Rather, it was the judgment of a personal God, who had orchestrated these events to bring about justice. The brothers would all have to become slaves as a just penalty for their sin of selling Joseph into slavery. Meanwhile, Joseph pretended not to understand Judah's words, insisting that only Benjamin was guilty and only he needed to pay. Instead of the punishment of death for the transgressor, Benjamin would be a slave in Egypt for the rest of his life, while the brothers could go back home in peace (*shalom*, verse 17).

A SUBSTITUTE PROVIDED

The situation was beautifully crafted to provide the perfect parallel to the brothers' earlier sin. The favored brother, Benjamin, would be left in Egypt as a slave, while the other brothers went home happily to their father, their sacks once again bulging with silver as well as the grain necessary for their survival. But these similarities set up the divergent ending to this story. At the crucial moment, Judah stepped forward and fulfilled the pledge he had made to his father (Gen. 43:9). The brother who first hatched the plan to sell Joseph as a slave had come full circle. He himself would stay in Benjamin's place because he could not bear to see the old man's sorrow if he were to be separated from Benjamin as well as Joseph. Earlier, the brothers had taken no thought for their father's feelings when they sold Joseph and sent his bloodied coat back home (37:32). But now they were changed men, and Judah could not imagine going home without Benjamin. Where would be the peace (*shalom*) in such a return?

It is little wonder that Joseph could not contain himself any longer. He broke down and wept and revealed himself to his brothers: "I am Joseph! Is my father still alive?" (Gen. 45:3). Their repentance paved the way for restoration and reconciliation. Because Judah was willing to suffer for a crime he did not commit, they were all forgiven for the crime that they did commit. That's quite a change for the Judah who a few years earlier had to confess that his prostitute-imitating Canaanite daughter-in-law was more righteous than he (38:26)! Joseph did not merely weep on Benjamin's neck; he now kissed and wept on all his brothers (45:15). All were included in the grand reconciliation, as the harmonious community of brothers that God had earlier promised to establish was finally being realized.

Joseph's ability to forgive his brothers is perhaps unmatched in the Old Testament. By their wickedness, the brothers caused him to be sold into slavery, so that the best years of his life were spent in various forms of servitude and imprisonment. That pain-filled experience was not quickly forgotten, as the names that he gave his sons bore vivid testimony (Gen. 41:51–52). Yet when God presented Joseph with a golden opportunity to make his brothers pay for their crime, he passed it up. He could have put his brothers into prison and left them to rot. Instead, he devised a complicated and costly plan for their redemption, enabling them to make a kind of restitution in the only way possible for their crime. It was a costly plan for him, but at the end of the journey he could welcome them back into his presence—not as his slaves, but as his family. They were reconciled.

LEARNING TO FORGIVE

How was Joseph able to forgive like this, when we so often are not? A key element was his ability to see clearly the overarching purpose of God: "God sent me before you to preserve life" (Gen. 45:5). He recognized that even when others sinned against him, God was still up to something good in his life and theirs. The brothers' sin turned out to be a crucial part of God's plan to provide food for his people through the famine, as well as bringing them down into Egypt, where the next chapter of their lives would play out. If we were able to recognize that God's gracious work continues even through the sins of others, we would learn better how to forgive.

Perhaps someone has sinned against you in deeply painful ways; can you see that since God always gets his way, and since he is always at work for good, this too must be something that he will work for your good? Perhaps your situation will enable you to see your own heart more clearly. Your trial may show you your desperate need of other believers and of God himself. That truth may encourage you along the costly path toward reconciliation.

Put like that, however, the whole process of forgiveness may seem rather easy and trite: remember that God is always up to something good when people sin against you, and you too will be able to forgive them like Joseph with a happy smile. In real life, of course, it is rarely that simple. For twenty years, Joseph couldn't see a single scrap of evidence that God was going to work his suffering for good. On the contrary, it must have seemed as if any hope of reconciliation with his brothers was unthinkable. So too, it may take a long time for you to see what God is accomplishing through the painful sins of others against you. God's plans for your good are not always simple and transparent. You may need others to come alongside you and help you to discern the fruit that God is bringing out of your life in the land of your affliction.

Nor should we miss the fact that God's wonderful plan to feed his people in Egypt also included the next step, which involved their experience of oppressive bondage under a Pharaoh who had forgotten Joseph (Ex. 1:8). Ironically, the slavery that Joseph did not demand for the brothers came upon a subsequent generation, which then in turn became the means for them to see the power of God at work in a new and amazing way in the Exodus! Far from bypassing suffering and victimization, God's wonderful plan for your life often takes you through the midst of pain and loss, just as it did for Jesus himself. Affliction is the soil in which the fruit of patience, endurance, perseverance, and hope most richly grow.

LEARNING TO BE FORGIVEN

Yet there is more to this story than learning how to forgive. It also shows us something profound about learning how to be forgiven. We instinctively want to identify with Joseph, the heroic forgiver of those who sinned against him. However, in many ways we are more like Joseph's

121

brothers; we are the ones who have betrayed and used others to achieve our own ends. Our jealousy has led us to murder others in our thoughts and in our words, through malicious gossip and explosive anger. Our lust has bought and sold our sisters and brothers in our minds, using them to satisfy our fantasies. Our *shalom* is deeply broken, our relationships are fractured, and our souls are tortured by the deep-rooted guilt that will not let us go, a scarlet stain that never disappears from our consciousness, no matter how hard we scrub. Perhaps you have committed sins today that press their claims against you, leaving you feeling constantly dirty and defiled. Who will step forward in our place to be our Judah and reconcile us to one another and to our Father?

That question reminds us that in Joseph's story there is a profound picture of God's love for us. Adam and Eve sinned against God and destroyed the harmony that had previously existed between God and man. God would have been entirely justified in destroying them then and there, or reducing them to the most abject form of slavery. We are no different from Adam. We have all sinned against God and against one another in thought, word, and deed, and daily continue to do so. Justice rightly demands death for our transgressions. But God did not pursue simple justice against us. Instead, he advanced a complicated and costly plan for our redemption, a plan that would both satisfy the claims of justice *and* allow us to receive the mercy and grace we need in order to be reconciled to him. God sent his only Son, Jesus, into this world of affliction and pain for us.

Jesus' love for us is far greater than Judah's love for his father. Jesus not only had to be willing to bear the punishment for another's sin, but also had to carry that willingness through to the end. Judah may have offered to be Joseph's slave, but Judah's greater Son actually bore the blame that we deserved. He came to bear a lifetime of limitation, sickness, rejection, and abuse. The Creator of all was rejected and scorned by his own people. The eternal Lord of Hosts took flesh and dwelt among us (John 1:14), subject to all the pains and weakness that come with that state. He willingly became a servant, in order to free us from our bondage to sin, death, and hell. Ultimately, he took that obedience all the way to the cross, where he bore the weight of divine rejection and torment that our sins deserved.

Jesus was born, suffered, died, and rose again as part of God's great plan, both to save the lives of his people through a great deliverance and to create a harmonious community of brothers and sisters through the suffering of a substitute. Here, too, God's good purpose was achieved through his sovereign control over men's sinful actions. Peter declared in his sermon on the day of Pentecost:

> This Jesus, delivered up according to the definite plan and foreknowledge of God, you crucified and killed by the hands of lawless men. God raised him up, loosing the pangs of death, because it was not possible for him to be held by it. (Acts 2:23–24)

What we meant for evil, God meant for good.

Not surprisingly, the news of their forgiveness was such stunning news to Joseph's brothers that they were unable at first to believe it. They remained terrified in his presence, expecting the ax to fall on their heads at any moment. But Joseph graciously told his brothers, "Do not be distressed or angry with yourselves because you sold me here" (Gen. 45:5). Joseph saw the dismay on their faces and knew that even though he had freely forgiven them, they would struggle to feel forgiven by him.

You and I may also struggle to feel forgiven by God, even though we are indeed forgiven for all of our sins— past, present, and future. Much of our lack of peace in the Christian life flows from that struggle. Because we don't feel forgiven, we search for peace by finding some way to prove that we really are worthy of God's love. We seek peace through acts of service or an endless cycle of Christian disciplines, but that is a losing battle. These things may be good in themselves, but they are not our peace. Our peace rests in knowing that God has forgiven us for the sake of our substitute, Jesus Christ. God therefore says to us too, "Do not be distressed or angry with yourself over your sin." The voice of condemnation comes from Satan, not from God. Yes, your sin is great and deep, and it matters. It is greater and deeper than you can even conceive, so great that nothing less than the death of the perfect Son of God could possibly pay for it. But through his death, the penalty is fully and finally paid. He stood condemned in your place and was executed for this particular sin of yours. So why do you keep trying to take back the place of condemnation that Jesus has taken for you? If God does not condemn you, why continue constantly to condemn yourself? Don't be slow to believe the good news about Jesus, even though it may seem too good to be true.

LIVING UNDER JOSEPH'S RULE

The test that Joseph's brothers now faced was whether they were willing to live under his rule. They had to choose between continued independence, which meant ongoing destitution in Canaan, and submitting themselves to a life of dependence upon Joseph's provisions in Egypt. The prospect of bowing down to their brother, as depicted in Joseph's earlier dreams, had now become a reality. Yet it must have been much easier for them to submit to the Joseph who had now demonstrated his love and care for them so richly and deeply than it would have been to submit to the brash and obnoxious youth who first proclaimed his dreams to them. It is the same for us. We have to choose between living spiritually destitute and broken lives here in this world apart from God and submitting to God and accepting his provision for our lives. Yet it makes all the difference to know that the God who calls us to submit to him is the same God who is rich in mercy and grace, and who has forgiven us so abundantly for our rebellion against him. Why would you continue to hold out against the God who has loved you so much in sending Christ to be your Savior? What is there to gain by resisting such a kind and gracious king?

This decision to submit our hearts to the Lord is not simply a one-time decision. It is a daily battle to believe that the one whom we have wronged, and continue to wrong, loves us so much that he is willing to forgive our sins and to provide us with everything that we need. Moreover, it is a daily battle for us to extend to others the same mercy and forgiveness that we ourselves have received.

Where could Joseph's brothers look for assurance that he really meant well for them? Surely the assurance was in the complicated plan of their salvation: if Joseph had meant to do them harm, he could easily have had them imprisoned or killed when they first arrived. He did not need to endure emotional pain merely to make them his slaves or to take their donkeys. Joseph had the power to impose swift justice on them. No one could have argued that such an action would have been unfair or unjust. Instead, Joseph launched his complex plan to enable them to demonstrate repentance and be reconciled to him. Someone who had gone to such lengths to win them back must surely have had their best interests at heart.

It is the same for us, whenever we are tempted to doubt whether God really is at work in this world for our good. As we face trials and temptations, and find ourselves wondering whether God is simply dealing with us as we deserve for all of our sins, the Father points us back to his complex plan of salvation. He demonstrated his self-sacrificial love in a plan that worked itself out over centuries and culminated in the gift of his own Son. This gift assures us of his good plans for our future. As Paul puts it in Romans 8:31–32,

> What then shall we say to these things? If God is for us, who can be against us? He who did not spare his own Son but gave him up for us all, how will he not also with him graciously give us all things?

Paradoxically, when we recognize that we are the brothers in this story, not Joseph, we actually begin to learn to forgive like Joseph. What could possibly motivate you to extend love and forgiveness and to seek costly reconciliation with people who have hurt you and harmed you so profoundly? It is as we ponder how greatly we ourselves have been forgiven and what a great price has been paid for our reconciliation that our hearts start to melt toward those who have so greatly sinned against us. Yes, justice demands that they should pay, just as it demands that we should pay. However, we have not received justice from God, but mercy—mercy that is deep and wide, as deep and wide as our sin. Our scarlet stains of sin have been washed whiter than snow through the substitute who bore the claims of justice in our place. Jesus has reconciled us to himself, and now he gently asks us to be reconciled to one another as a harmonious family of brothers and sisters, forgiving others with the same measure of forgiveness that we have received. What is more, he calls us to lift our eyes upward to our heavenly home, the place where all of our broken relationships will finally and fully be reconciled, just as we are reconciled even now to God himself.

FOR FURTHER REFLECTION

1. How was the brothers' guilt revealed? What did confrontation with guilt reveal about the brothers?

2. Jesus offered himself as a substitute, both to save his people from their guilt and to create a harmonious community. How does this story demonstrate the connection between personal and relational renewal? Do you tend to emphasize one of those elements at the expense of the other? How and why?

3. As they lived under Joseph's authority, what assurance did the brothers have of his favor? How do you resist God's authority? What assurance do you have of his favor?

CHAPTER TEN

FROM FAMINE TO FORTUNE (GENESIS 45:16–46:27)

How often and how intensely are you hungry? For most of us, the combination of the agricultural revolution, efficient systems of distribution, and a social safety net have nearly eliminated severe hunger and famine. In fact, attention has now shifted to a national crisis of obesity. But in missed corners of developed societies or in the widespread plight of emerging nations, painful hunger remains persistent. For others of us, the idea of hunger sends our thoughts not to an empty feeling in the pit of our stomach, but to an empty gnawing in our soul. You may have met all of your physical needs for food, shelter, and clothing, and may even enjoy success and a good reputation. Yet there is an emptiness and a restlessness nonetheless. You may look outside yourself and see a world that isn't right, or inside yourself and see shocking ugliness. What did Jesus mean when he said, "Blessed are those who hunger and thirst for righteousness, for they shall be satisfied" (Matt. 5:6)? Whether you are scaling the ladder of success or struggling to survive, Genesis 45 and 46 point you to a God who keeps his promises to his people and brings them from famine to fortune.

THE SHADOW

Thus far in the story, Jacob's family has faced two distinct but equally dangerous problems. Either one could have undermined God's promise to Abraham to bless not only his family but all of the nations of the world through them (Gen. 12:1–3). The first problem was internal. Although God had repeatedly promised to make Abraham's family into a great nation, domestic dysfunction among Jacob, Joseph, and Joseph's brothers came close to sinking the entire project. Alongside that danger was a second, external threat: the seven-year famine throughout the entire region of Egypt and Canaan.

In only the second year of the famine, Jacob's sons were already desperate enough to have embarked on two separate journeys from Canaan to Egypt. Jacob did not want to send his new favorite son, Benjamin, on the first journey because of the dangers that it entailed. The desperation was even greater for the second trip. The "lord of the land" had told them to bring back their youngest brother as proof that they were telling the truth, and they had been forced to leave Simeon in Egypt as a hostage (Gen. 42:19–20). What kind of reception could they expect, having failed to return thus far? They had no choice but to run that risk, because they were facing a literal life-or-death situation. As Jacob said before the first journey, "Go down and buy grain for us there, that we may live and not die" (42:2). Joseph sent them home with grain for their families, so that "you shall not die" (42:19–20). When Judah urged Jacob to release Benjamin for the second journey, it was so that "we may live and not die, both we and you and also our little ones" (43:8). Jacob's family had been living under the shadow of death.

Whether or not we have experienced severe hunger, we are all more or less familiar with life under the shadow of death. One person's brush with death may be profound and protracted: "There's a mass. It may be cancer." Your encounter may have been less sharp, but still attention grabbing. At a presurgery consultation for the removal of wisdom teeth, my wife's dentist mentioned offhand that, as safe as anesthesia may be, it does not matter much if you are the one in ten thousand who dies. That observation bothered her less than it bothered me when I had my own wisdom teeth extracted a few months later. Your confrontation with death may have come through a painful sickness or the loss of a friend, child, or spouse. Despite our best efforts as individuals and as a culture to avoid thinking about death, it is ever present. Perhaps fittingly, the seminary I attended overlooked a cemetery, and there are two funeral homes in the neighborhood in which we live. We all know what it is like to live in the shadow of death, whether from hunger, illness, or freak accident.

As famine gripped the land of Canaan, that shadow of death hung over Jacob's family. That danger made the reversal of their fortunes, as recorded in this chapter, all the more breathtaking. "The sons of Israel," we read in Genesis 42:5, "came to buy among the others who came, for the famine was in the land of Canaan." God's chosen family had been reduced to just one more group of wandering refugees, seeking food in order to survive. But now, following the revelation of Joseph's identity, that very family was quickly elevated from poverty to riches. The hungry wanderers enjoyed royal favor, riches, and welcome.

THE INVITATION

Our passage opens with Pharaoh hearing that Joseph's family has come. Pharaoh's favor rested on Joseph for good cause. Because of Joseph, there was still food in Egypt. It had been stockpiled at Joseph's suggestion during the seven plentiful years. In gratitude for how God had blessed his kingdom through Joseph, Pharaoh invited Joseph's entire extended family to live in the shelter of Egypt for the remainder of the famine. Pharaoh promised "the best of the land" and "the fat of the land" (Gen. 45:18). He encouraged the family to leave behind their old belongings, for the best things in all the land of Egypt would be theirs. Their new homes would be fully furnished with all that they required. It was as if they had won the ultimate extreme makeover.

Joseph himself gave them abundant provisions for the journey. Earlier they had been irrationally afraid that Joseph was going to steal their donkeys (Gen. 43:18); instead, Joseph gave them twenty *extra* donkeys for the trip home (45:23). Benjamin received twenty-two years' worth of deferred birthday money in the form of three hundred pieces of silver, while each of the brothers was given a new suit (45:22). Notice how that brings everything full circle. Twenty years before, Joseph's fancy clothes had incited the brothers' jealousy and bitterness. Once they got rid of Joseph, they used that very garment to convince their father that Joseph was dead, torn to pieces by a wild animal. While Jacob tore his clothes in mourning, the brothers watched, completely unmoved. But all these years later, the brothers demonstrated changed hearts. Despite Benjamin being the new favorite, they did not take advantage of a convenient opportunity to dispose of him. Instead, they tore *their* clothes (44:13). They mourned over God's exposure of their guilt, and they dreaded to see the anguish that their father would feel if they were again to cause him to lose his beloved son.

Joseph's gift was a reminder of how comprehensively he had covered over their original sin against him. He was now covering the cost of *his* test and *their* repentance. He replaced their old, torn garments with brand-new apparel. So they all headed home, richly laden, with all their new belongings packed on top of Pharaoh's own wagons. Apparently these were extremely impressive wagons, as they are mentioned four times (Gen. 45:19, 21, 27; 46:5)—the ancient equivalent of luxury SUVs with black-tinted windows. The brothers who were on the edge of poverty and starvation had now become part of Pharaoh's entourage.

THE ANNOUNCEMENT

The reversal of their fortunes as they returned to Canaan set the stage for an even more startling reversal for Jacob. Remember, he was waiting at home for news while all of these events unfolded. How must it have felt to hear the announcement, "Joseph is still alive, and he is ruler over all the land of Egypt" (Gen. 45:26)? Their news was so astonishing that, at first, Jacob could not believe it. He feared that his sorrow would bring him to the grave, yet it was actually the shock of unbelievably good news that almost finished him off.

The whole exchange highlights God's transformation of this once-fractured family. But there was a great deal that was not said. There were no arguments about the original betrayal of Joseph, probably in response to Joseph's instructions: "Do not quarrel on the way" (Gen. 45:24). They had repented; Joseph had forgiven them. It was over and done.[1] But something else is missing from this conversation: Pharaoh's promise of wonderful new possessions. That seems like it would be a noteworthy piece of information: "Dad, we were going broke, but now we are rich!" Instead, both the brothers' report and Jacob's response focused on one thing: the life and well-being of the once-lost Joseph. That represented an immense change, not only in the brothers, but also in Jacob.

Jacob's personal history was full of underhanded efforts to achieve blessing at the expense of others. On two separate occasions, he swindled his slightly older twin brother Esau: first out of the birthright and then out of the blessing of the firstborn (Gen. 25:29–34; 27:1–41). Jacob swindled his uncle Laban out of his flocks (30:25–43). He even tried to wrestle a blessing out of God himself (32:22–32). Jacob's powers of deception were astonishing, although they were appropriate in view of the fact that the name Jacob means "he deceives." One of the darker strains of Jacob's character was his overwhelming focus on tangible, physical blessing: the beautiful wife, the abundant children, status, and riches. Even when he had those things, he was not a particularly good husband or father. Yet with the recovery of Joseph, we see evidence that God had finally begun to reorient Jacob's distorted priorities.

The abundant tokens of the family's newfound status now served a different purpose. Why did Joseph load up his brothers with all those riches if he simply wanted them to bring Jacob back to Egypt? Why not just park the extra donkeys in the multi-stall garage at the new family estate? Joseph sent those gifts as tokens confirming the truth of the brothers' incredible report. On its own, "Joseph is alive and lord of Egypt" was an unbelievable, too-good-to-be-true story. But those royal wagons were visible, tangible evidence that this impossible story had to be true (Gen. 45:27). Even then, Jacob's heart remained fixed, not on the tangible royal gifts, but on what they pointed to: his son's life. "It is enough; Joseph my son is still alive. I will go and see him before I die" (45:28). God completely reversed Jacob's expectations from over twenty years before, when he said, "I shall go down to Sheol to my son, mourning" (37:35). Contrary to his expectations, Jacob and Joseph would be reunited, not in the land of the dead, but in the land of the living!

There is more to this narrative than just a good "rags to riches" story. The famine-to-fortune story of Joseph's family points forward to our own famine-to-fortune story. In Luke's gospel, Jesus says to all who hear him: "Blessed are you who are poor, for yours is the kingdom of God. Blessed are you who are hungry now, for you shall be satisfied. Blessed are you who weep now, for you shall laugh" (Luke 6:20–21). Through Christ, the good report to Jacob echoes into each of our lives as we struggle under the shadow of death. The Son who was dead is now alive. He is the Lord of the land, the Crown Prince of all creation! Jesus has absorbed the cost of our sin against him. If you belong to him, he has forgiven your sins and has covered and clothed you in his righteousness. Jesus has freed you from the endless cycle of accusation, guilt, and self-defense, of sin, shame, and suffering. Because the Father is pleased with Jesus, we are welcomed into his kingdom. God the Father and Jesus the Lord have summoned us into an inheritance of royal richness, from which not even death can separate us. While we await our inheritance, we are given everything that we need to bring us safely there. Like Pharaoh's wagons, the Spirit confirms the truth of our invitation and brings us into the resurrection life of Jesus that we are invited to share.

Jacob's response to the announcement of Joseph's "resurrection" was remarkably similar to the apostles' response to reports of the resurrection of Jesus: a mix of unbelief and belief, doubt and faith. To aid our faith, Jesus surrounds us with tokens of his reality and his grace, tokens that testify that because Jesus has burst the bonds of death, we will one day see him face-to-face in the true "land of the living." However terrible your circumstances feel right now, they are not the last word. They are only a fleeting reality.

THE CONFIRMATION

As chapter 46 opens, God confirms to Jacob that he is trustworthy. God will be faithful to his promises. On his way to Egypt, Jacob stopped at Beersheba to worship God. Beersheba is at the southernmost edge of the Promised Land. In the film *The Fellowship of the Ring*, there is a point where Samwise Gamgee stops and tells Frodo, "This is it. If I take one more step, it'll be the farthest away from home I've ever been."[2] Passing that particular spot marked for Sam a decisive break with the past and a leap into an unknown future. Likewise, Jacob was about to break with his past. Famine to fortune sounded fabulous, except it involved the family going in what appeared to be the wrong direction—out of the Promised Land to live in Egypt. God had told Jacob, when he gave him his new name Israel, "The land that I gave to Abraham and Isaac I will give to you, and I will give the land to your offspring after you" (Gen. 35:12).

Here, after decades of silence, God graciously confirmed to Jacob that his plan was still on schedule. Indeed, in Genesis 15:13–14, God had told Abraham that his offspring would sojourn in a distant land and be afflicted for four hundred years, after which he would bring them out with great possessions. The reiteration of that promise to Jacob was not only an encouragement to him, but also to the first readers of this story. The nation of Israel, after the exodus and before the conquest, needed to hear this reminder of God's faithfulness. If Jacob felt that he was going the wrong way, they often must have felt that they were going nowhere, as they wandered in the wilderness.

That may sound familiar to many subsequent readers, including us. We too may feel that we are going in the wrong way or nowhere at all. Sometimes, like Jacob, we find ourselves facing a fork in the road, and it looks like we have to choose either the way of obedience or the way of blessing and happiness. Why is our journey to receive what God has promised so circuitous? What does God have against taking the easy route?

In such times, we need to keep two things clearly in mind. We have seen God's plan to alleviate tangible, physical threats to his people, like the famine, but he also has other goals in mind. Some of those aims concerning the future of Israel will come into view in the next chapter. Yet looking back through Genesis, we can see how every advance of God's overall plan for his people also weaves together important changes in their individual lives. The trip to Egypt, in particular, brings this intricacy of God's plans to the fore.

Remember what happened to Abraham almost immediately after he first received God's promise. In response to a famine, he went down to Egypt and acted in a manner completely antithetical to that promise (Gen. 12:10–20). Instead of blessing his host nation, Abraham misrepresented his relationship to Sarah out of fear for himself. He allowed Pharaoh's unwitting acquisition of the already-married Sarah, which led to Abraham's enrichment, but also to a curse falling upon Pharaoh, his host. That was not a great start to being a blessing to all nations! Later, during another famine, God told Isaac outright: "Do not go down to Egypt: dwell in the land of which I shall tell you" (26:2). So Isaac traveled to the Philistine city of Gerar—where, however, he copied his father's example of claiming that his wife was his sister. For Abraham and Isaac, these experiences revealed that their fear of men and their love of safety were stronger than their trust in God and their love for their wives and their hosts.

Jacob, on the other hand, kept trying to force God's hand and acquire the promised blessings through his own efforts. But God changed him, so that he was actually willing to leave the Promised Land and trust that God would eventually bring his family back. Whether one is going or coming, Egypt generally reveals more about the spiritual condition and personal idolatries of each individual or generation than anything else. Likewise, depending on the person concerned, God can use the very same circumstance to teach two people completely different things. He can also challenge the same idolatry in two different hearts in widely different situations.

When we face our toughest dilemmas, the urgent question on our lips is usually, "What does God want me to do?" Instead, we should probably ask, "What is God revealing to me about my heart? How is he using this issue to uncover the distance between my values and his?" For example, my wife and I, having small children, will have to make important choices about their education. Should we choose public school, private school, or home school? As we consider that decision, God is revealing something about our hearts. I wrestle with the idol of educational achievement as a vehicle for worldly success. There is also my arrogant tendency to be contrary and want to do something different from what other people think is the "obvious" right answer. There are even my conflicting idolatries of convenience (there is a Christian school across the street from our home) and financial freedom (public school is free). There is so much more to this decision than simply the decision itself.

God's diverse handling of the differing idolatries of Abraham, Isaac, and Jacob points to another tendency that we may have. Once we are convinced what God has called us to do, we may try to impose the answer in our situation on everyone else, regardless of their situation. Yet their circumstances may be quite different, and God may be up to something very different in their lives. For someone else, the same decision could reveal different idolatries and suggest that different choices should be made.

Something else to consider, when we struggle with God's circuitous plans for our lives, is that God doesn't exempt himself from that struggle. When Satan offered to give Jesus all the kingdoms of this world, Jesus could easily have felt that he faced the choice between the way of obedience and the way of blessing and happiness. Had he not come to rule the kingdoms of this world? Satan appeared to offer a route to receive the kingdom without the pain of the cross. But Jesus did not take the path without pain, because a kingdom without a cross would have been a kingdom without forgiveness and salvation. Jesus' mission was not only to receive a kingdom, but also to save sinners and bring glory to the Father by creating a new humanity.

THE MIGRATION

That new humanity is anticipated in the final section of this passage, which lists all of the individuals who migrated from Canaan to Egypt. Unless you're a member of the American Genealogical Society, an extensive list of names may seem about as interesting as reading the phone book. Yet they are there for a reason. Like the other genealogies in Genesis, this list is a turning point in the book of Genesis as a whole. Here the story of Jacob's family in Palestine is coming to a close, and the remainder of the book will be focused on the early days of Israel's sojourn in Egypt.

However, this family list also highlights the first flowering of God's promise to Abraham. We finally see the unfolding of God's promise to make Abraham's children into a great nation. Who would have thought, years before, that Abraham and Sarah, an elderly and barren couple, would give rise to *any* family, let alone seventy people? Moreover, in the overarching story of Genesis, it is no accident that there are seventy. The seventy members of the family of Israel echo the seventy nations of the world that descended from Noah (see Genesis 10). In the midst of these nations, God is preparing a new people who will carry his promises.

Of course, following somebody else's family tree can be even more boring than reading the phone book. But if it is your own family, it becomes a different matter. Later Israelites could look at this list and see what God had continued to do. From a barren couple to a family of seventy may seem miraculous, but God continued to do wonders. Even when Pharaoh attempted to eradicate God's family in Egypt (see Exodus 1), they continued to increase and multiply. The first edition of Genesis was read to hundreds of thousands of people who could say, "Look at what God has done!"

We can say the same thing, because this is also our family history. In Jesus, Christians have been grafted into that family tree, adopted into Abraham's family. Look at what God has done! Right now there are hundreds of millions of Christians, perhaps billions, who are brothers and sisters in Jesus. In each of our local church families, we get to be God's welcoming party in our little corner of the world as he continues to grow that family, whether through conversions, recommitments, or newborn children.

The list of Jacob's family also highlights the diversity of people whom God calls into his family. When everyone arrived in Egypt, it would have been a rather odd family reunion. Some were rich and influential, like Joseph. Others were nobodies: people like Jahzeel, Guni, Jezer, and Shillem—or any of the many other people that we never hear mentioned in Scripture again. There were inept misfits like Reuben, efficient swindlers like Jacob, and those with a history of sexual sin like Judah, but God was working in each one of them. It is the same in the church. In God's providence, you may be from an inbred, redneck family like Perez and Zerah, or one of the kids from a big-city, biracial marriage like Ephraim and Manasseh. It doesn't matter. Everyone who loves Jesus is welcome in God's family.

All around the world, God is using his new family to bring men, women, and children from famine to fortune. Like Joseph, we are called to reflect a little bit of what God has done for us in Jesus. Like Joseph, some may be able to alleviate the shadow of death through wise public policy. Others may be able to send financial help around the world to where people are hungry, hurting, or suffering. Some may be able to go themselves to serve, whether short-term or long-term. Some have opportunities to open their own homes and show hospitality to people in need in our families, our church, and our community. Nearly every church has people in need as well as those who are eager to come alongside the hungry and hurting to provide practical, emotional, and spiritual help. What is more, every believer, from the richest to the poorest, has the opportunity and the joy to share the good report that

Jesus is alive. He is the Lord of all creation, who invites us out of our famine and need into the glorious place he has prepared for us! When the shadow of death has finally passed, we shall be there with him forever.

FOR FURTHER REFLECTION

1. What external and internal problems threatened to undermine God's promises to Joseph's family? How did God's circuitous plan for Joseph's family address those threats? How did it prepare Israel for the future?

2. Joseph sent tangible evidence to confirm to Jacob that he really was alive. In what tangible ways does God remind us that Jesus really lives?

3. How have you seen God use the same difficult decisions to teach different things to different people? Do you expect others to learn the same lessons as you from similar experiences?

4. The large company migrating to Egypt reminds us that God kept his promises to Abraham's family despite the dysfunction in Jacob's family. How has God been faithful to his promises despite the presence of sin in your life, family, church, or community?

CHAPTER ELEVEN

BETTER THAN WE DESERVE (GENESIS 46:28–47:31)

"How are you doing?" That's the kind of greeting we sometimes give each other without expecting a profound answer. I often respond to it with an ambiguous "Fine." On some days, that means "I'm doing quite well today"; on other days, it is an acronym for "Frantic, Insecure, Neurotic, and Exhausted." I just don't have the energy to go into detail about my problems, and you probably don't want to know anyway. In my former church in California, there was a young man who, whenever you asked him how he was doing, would reply, "Better than I deserve." That is certainly accurate as a description of how Jacob and his sons were doing at this point in the story. Joseph's brothers had gone on their second trip to Egypt in desperation, hoping just to be able to buy sufficient grain on which to survive until the famine was over. Perhaps they would even be able to get their imprisoned brother Simeon released. But they did not get what they bargained for—they got so much more! Instead of merely getting enough grain to stay alive, they were told to bring their whole family down to Egypt, so that they could live on the fat of the land (Gen. 45:18). They did not merely get Simeon back and return Benjamin safely to his father;

they also received the news that Joseph was alive—and the ruler of all Egypt! The brothers were treated far better than they deserved.

So too was Jacob. He let Simeon rot in an Egyptian dungeon, rather than risk his beloved Benjamin. After Benjamin's departure for Egypt, Jacob lived on a knife edge of fear, wondering if he would ever see him again. Not only did Benjamin return safely, but Jacob received Joseph back as well, as if from the dead. The donkeys that went off, bearing a small gift for the mysterious ruler of Egypt, returned pulling carts laden with the best things of Egypt—proof that the brothers' incredible news was true.

That is a wonderful picture of how God deals with us. When we come to God through Christ, we don't get what we deserve. We get far more than we could ever have imagined. We are forgiven for all of our sins and transgressions, adopted into God's family as sons and daughters, made co-heirs with Jesus Christ of a glorious eternal inheritance (Rom. 8:17), and thus made more than conquerors in life and in death (Rom. 8:37). Even here on earth, we sometimes experience the rich bounty of God's provision, so that we can say with the psalmist, "The lines have fallen for me in pleasant places; indeed, I have a beautiful inheritance" (Ps. 16:6). We have a great deal for which to be thankful.

Yet our hearts are often blind to God's mercy and grace. We moan and complain about anything that is wrong with our lives instead of celebrating and being thankful for what is right. I certainly do. I take for granted the many rich blessings God has given me and fixate on any aspect of my life that isn't the way I would like it to be. At work, I ignore everything I love about where God has placed me and complain about the relatively few negative elements (such as grading papers and quizzes). At home, I forget all of the great aspects of life with my wife and children and grumble in my heart about the little things they do that bother me. I regularly forget all of the ways in which God has placed me in a pleasant place and murmur instead about some little thing he has withheld.

Our grumbling hearts lead us to ponder the central element of this passage: Jacob's encounter with Pharaoh. When Pharaoh asked Jacob how old he was, he probably intended it merely as a polite conversation starter, an ancient "How are you doing?" In a society that venerated age, this was an invitation for Jacob to boast a little. Yet in response, Jacob told him, "The days of the years of my sojourning are 130 years. Few and evil have been the days of the years of my life, and they have not attained to the days of the years of the life of my fathers in the days of their sojourning" (Gen. 47:9). Given the opportunity to bear testimony to the Lord's power and grace before the most powerful man in the world, it seems that all Jacob could muster was, "My life has been nasty, brutish, and short." Well, not quite. There is actually more to this statement than meets the eye, and when we explore the ways in which Jacob is profoundly right, as well as the ways in which he is profoundly wrong, we can see how those perspectives should shape our own response to both good times and difficult times in our own lives.

HOW JACOB WAS WRONG

First, let's think about some of the ways in which Jacob was profoundly wrong when he said, "The days of my sojourning have been few and evil." To begin with, he was not dead yet, nor was it time for him to die. Yet his impending death had been on his mind for some time. When he saw Joseph's bloodstained robe, he was sure he was about to go down to Sheol in sorrow (Gen. 37:35). When the brothers wanted to take Benjamin down to Egypt on the second trip, Jacob's concern was that if anything happened to his son on the journey, it would kill him (42:38). When Jacob heard that Joseph was still alive, he declared that he would go to see him before he died (45:28). Even when he finally saw him, he said, "Now let me die, since I have seen your face and know that you are still alive" (46:30). Yet Jacob still had another seventeen years to live in Joseph's company (47:28), the same length of time that he spent with Joseph during the first years of his life. As Mark Twain might have put it, the reports of Jacob's impending death were greatly exaggerated.

It is interesting to speculate whether Jacob's description of his life would have been different if he had met Pharaoh after those last seventeen peaceful years, rather than before them. His dying words in chapters 48 and 49 suggest so. Either way, his statement shows us someone so turned in on himself by a life-shattering event that he had lost the ability to recognize anything else that God had given him. God had intervened in Jacob's situation and dramatically turned it around, and yet it seemed that Jacob was still determined to define his life by his pain, rather than by God's redemption of that pain. He had been deeply and painfully sinned against, and that had become the defining story of his life.

what defines you?

Nor does it seem that there was any ownership of the part that Jacob's own sin had played in making his life miserable. To be sure, others had sinned against him in significant ways. His father, Isaac, had favored his older brother, Esau, creating deep family rivalry. Esau wanted to kill Jacob, forcing him to flee from his home and family. His uncle Laban had deceived him and abused his trust, marrying him first to unwanted Leah and then using him as cheap labor to care for his flocks. Finally, Jacob's own sons had deceived him and stolen Joseph away. Yet Jacob had not exactly been an innocent bystander in his own life, merely observing as bad things happened to him. He had been an active participant in each of those situations, sinning as well as being sinned against, making for himself much of the trouble that would return on his own head.

In light of that reality, it would seem that a more sober evaluation would have been that Jacob's life had actually turned out much better than he deserved. Look at all of the ways in which God had fulfilled his promises to him: from wandering at Bethel, fleeing his home with nothing but a walking stick, Jacob had now become the patriarch of a family of seventy persons. God was fulfilling his promise to make him into a great nation. What is more, God was protecting and providing richly for that nation. The Lord sent Joseph ahead of them to Egypt and raised him to this position of leadership, so that Israel would be kept alive and not die. God's incredibly generous provision for his people is a key theme in this passage. When Joseph's brothers appeared before Pharaoh, he told Joseph to settle his family in the best land of Egypt (Gen. 47:6)—a command that Joseph faithfully followed (47:11). They received a pleasant place to live in the land of Goshen, where they could safely and comfortably raise their flocks and their families.

Their life in Egypt during this time was also significantly better than that of the native population. During the famine, the rest of Egypt was desperate for food, to the point that they sold their land, their cattle, and themselves to Pharaoh, becoming his indentured servants (Gen. 47:20–21). They ended up working land that had formerly been theirs, but now with the requirement to send a fifth of the produce to Pharaoh in token of his ownership. The Egyptians were grateful for this agreement, for by it Joseph preserved their lives, just as he had preserved the lives of his own family (47:25). Indeed, by ancient standards it was a modest rate; the average was around a third.[1] But this slavery and bondage for the Egyptians in their own land contrasted sharply with the freedom and prosperity of Jacob's family. Though strangers and aliens in the land of Egypt, they were granted an inheritance there by Joseph (47:11) and do not seem to have had to come repeatedly to their brother to beg for food. For the Israelites of Moses' day, it must have seemed strange to remember a time when they were the prosperous class in Egypt and the Egyptians were in bondage, rather than vice versa.

Before Jacob left the Promised Land, God promised to be with him and go down to Egypt with him (Gen. 46:4). Without that, all of the other blessings would not have been enough. The blessing of God's presence and favor, the blessing for which Jacob had struggled all of his life, continued to rest upon him, in spite of his continued sinfulness and self-centeredness. In fact, the Lord even promised that Joseph's hand would close Jacob's eyes (46:4). In spite of Jacob's idolatrous focus on Joseph, God did not snatch away the object of his idolatry. Instead, he mercifully promised him the comfort of having his favorite son with him at the end. God certainly dealt with Jacob far better than he deserved.

Could Jacob not see anything of God's goodness in all of this? Joseph could say to his brothers, "You meant it for evil but God meant it for good" (see Gen. 50:20), but Jacob could only get as far as "You meant it for evil." Yet aren't we often like Jacob? It is easy for us to look around the circumstances of our lives and see all of the ways in which they are not what we had hoped. Perhaps you long to be married, or to have children, or to have a better marriage, or easier children. Maybe you wish for more money to pay your bills, or more time to spend with your family, or less time to spend by yourself. Perhaps you are praying to be delivered from a life-defining struggle or besetting sin. The list of things that we want goes on and on, and it is not necessarily a list of trivial or evil desires. Our list is often peopled with good things that we desire and genuine evils from which we want to be delivered.

Perhaps you have prayed over that list for years, asking God to give you these particular blessings and to free you from these pains. Yet in the process of thinking about all of the aspects of your situation that have not worked out the way you wanted them to, have you missed the good things God is doing in you, as well as all of his blessings that you take for granted? It is just as true for you as it was for Joseph and Jacob that the things others mean for evil, God means for good. None of your pains, your trials, your frustrated hopes, or your difficulties are wasted in God's wisdom. If it were good for you to have the things for which you long, our merciful and generous God would freely give them to you. Perhaps he will give them to you in the future, in a way that will make it all the more evident that they are gifts from him. Perhaps, in his incredible grace, your Joseph will be the one to close your eyes as God grants you at last the longing of your heart. Or perhaps he will strengthen you to be able to live without these good gifts and to testify nonetheless in the midst of that absence that God himself is enough. Perhaps he will give you the grace to endure a lifelong struggle for contentment as you wrestle with an unruly heart that does not easily submit to God's wisdom and find that God's incredible grace is once again extended to you in the midst of your constant griping and complaining. Perhaps even today he will enable you to look around and see some tokens of his undeserved love for you in the people he has brought into your life and the good things that he has actually given you. Even while recognizing the deep and profound challenges of our lives, we may still confess that God has actually treated us far better than we deserve.

HOW JACOB WAS RIGHT

Yet that is not the whole story. Jacob was not completely wrong in his assessment of his life as nasty, brutish, and short. There are some ways in which that characterization was profoundly right. Jacob had truly suffered greatly in his life. Joseph was not the only one who had been dealing with a life of intense pain for the past twenty years;

Jacob too had been profoundly grieving. Nor was his life an easy ride before that. In some ways, Jacob's journey was far harder than the path God laid out for his father, Isaac, and perhaps even than that of his grandfather, Abraham. Jacob was not dead yet, but his life would indeed be shorter than that of the other patriarchs: 147 years, compared to 175 for Abraham and 180 for Isaac.

Perhaps because of what he had suffered, Jacob rightly characterized his experience of life here on earth as a sojourn. There was a key shift between Pharaoh's question and Jacob's answer. Pharaoh asked, "How many are the days of the years of your *life?*" But Jacob responded, "The days of the years of my *sojourning* are 130 years" (Gen. 47:8–9). Jacob knew that his time here on earth was not his life; it was merely a sojourn, a temporary stay somewhere, not a permanent residence. He had bounced around from the Promised Land to Paddan-aram, back to the Promised Land, and now down to Egypt. Even though Egypt would probably provide, over the next seventeen years, the best living situation that Jacob had ever experienced, it would never be home. The Lord who promised to go down to Egypt with him had also promised to bring him back up to Canaan (46:4). The departure of Jacob and his family from the Promised Land was only temporary, which is why Jacob made Joseph swear that after his death he would not bury him in Egypt, but would take his body back to the family plot at Machpelah (47:29–31).

Joseph also recognized that the family's time in Egypt was a sojourn, not an arrival at their permanent destination. That was why Joseph carefully scripted the brothers' encounter with Pharaoh, making sure that they would be settled safely in Goshen, on the sidelines of Egyptian life, where they could pursue their livelihood as shepherds, which was an abomination to the Egyptians (Gen. 47:1–4). He did not want them to get drawn into Egyptian life, but rather to stay on the margins, so they would be ready to leave when God called. Best of all, Goshen was on the eastern edge of Egypt, conveniently situated for when they finally made their exodus.

This challenges us to consider how we think about the days of the years of our lives. If our time here on earth is all that there is, and this world is our true home, then it makes perfect sense for us to be devastated when we don't get what we want. If this world is our life, and if our days are few and evil, then we have lost at the only game that really counts. But if this world is not our true home, but merely a temporary stopping place on the journey to our heavenly home, then that puts an entirely different perspective on both our present sufferings and our present glories.

We understand this when it comes to earthly journeys. If a snowstorm descends while you are traveling and you are forced to take refuge in a cheap hotel, you don't complain about the color scheme of the room or head to the local store to replace the shower curtain and drapes. You remember that you are only going to be there for a night or two. You can put up with almost anything for a couple of nights, knowing that after that you will be able to go home and laugh about your experience. Alternatively, if you are traveling on business and are given an upgraded suite in a luxurious hotel, you can enjoy it for a night or two without being fooled into thinking that the wonderful amenities are now your permanent right. Marble bathrooms, plush robes, and daily maid service may be lovely, but they are only temporary.

So too, this world is not our true home; it is a temporary stopping place on our greater journey. Our joys here may give us reasons to be thankful to the God from whom all good things flow, but they are not what define us. Our sufferings and disappointments here may bring tears to our eyes and sorrow to our hearts, but we remember that joy will come in the morning (Ps. 30:5). When we reach our true destination, those tears will be wiped away, and those sorrows will be comforted. In the meantime, these sufferings and disappointments come to us from the same hand that gives us our blessings, as an expression of the same fatherly wisdom that knows exactly what we need to experience in order to grow in our knowledge of our own hearts and our faith and dependence upon him.

The second thing Jacob was right about was his desire to see God's promise fulfilled. You can hear that longing in what he said when he finally saw Joseph: "Now let me die, since I have seen your face and know that you are still alive" (Gen. 46:30). That is almost exactly what aged Simeon said when they put the baby Jesus in his arms:

> Lord, now you are letting your servant depart in peace,
>   according to your word;
> for my eyes have seen your salvation
>   that you have prepared in the presence of all peoples,
> a light for revelation to the Gentiles,
>   and for glory to your people Israel. (Luke 2:29–32)

There is the same kind of messianic ring to what Jacob was saying, reinforcing the impression that what he saw in Joseph was the product of more than simple parental affection. He had pinned on Joseph all of his hopes of seeing God's promise to Abraham fulfilled.

The idea was natural since Joseph was the firstborn son of Jacob's favorite wife, Rachel. That was why he singled out Joseph in the first place to receive the specially decorated coat (Gen. 37:3). It must have been reinforced by Joseph's dreams, which depicted him receiving homage, not just from his brothers and parents, but even from the entire universe—the sun, moon and stars. These dreams provoked jealousy in his brothers, but Jacob "kept the saying in mind" (37:11). Surely that is why Jacob took Joseph's apparent death so badly, refusing to be comforted by his other children. Mourning the loss of a son is natural; however, unrestrained and inconsolable mourning signals that something else is at work. But now Jacob and Joseph were reunited. They embraced and wept, and Jacob declared, "Now let me die, since I have seen your face and know that you are still alive" (46:30). Why should Jacob have been so ready to die, unless he had seen his hopes for the fulfillment of God's blessing to Abraham restored?

Jacob's expectation that the promise would be passed on through Joseph was entirely reasonable and sensible—and entirely wrong. Joseph is the hero of the story, the most spotless character we have met in the book of Genesis, and the firstborn son of the beloved wife; surely he was the ideal man to carry the Abrahamic blessing. Yet God determined that the line of promise should descend not according to human merit, but rather according to grace. The line through which the Messiah would come would not consist of spotless heroes; rather, it would go through the immoral union of Judah with Tamar, his Canaanite daughter-in-law, whom Judah had mistaken for a prostitute (Gen. 38).

God wanted to make it clear that his choice of those whom he calls to be his servants is not based on performance. He can use the good and the bad alike. Entry to his kingdom is not limited to exemplary characters like Joseph; it is open to tax collectors and sinners, prostitutes, drug addicts, and gang members. It is even open to people like me: an arrogant overachiever, who is often far too impressed with his own performance. The promise of the Holy Spirit is extended to "everyone whom the Lord our God calls to himself" (Acts 2:39). So there is no room for pride. God did not choose you because you are cleverer or more moral than your neighbor; it is all of grace. As Paul puts it,

> But God chose what is foolish in the world to shame the wise; God chose what is weak in the world to shame the strong; God chose what is low and despised in the world, even things that are not, to bring to nothing things that are, so that no human being might boast in the presence of God. (1 Cor. 1:27–29)

The reverse side of that is that there is no room for favoritism. The message of the kingdom is to be preached freely to all alike: rich and poor, moral and immoral, influential and powerless. We, in our limited wisdom, might favor a Joseph, where God, in his infinite wisdom, has chosen to save a Judah.

PASSING ON THE BLESSING

Even while Jacob was completely wrong in thinking that the blessing would pass through the line of Joseph, he was entirely right in his confidence that there was a blessing to be passed on. Here was a man who had been rendered virtually penniless by famine, the head of a tiny family of seminomadic shepherds. Yet when he met Pharaoh, the mightiest man in the world, it was Jacob who blessed Pharaoh and not vice versa. What chutzpah! In the ancient world, the greater person always blessed the lesser. How audacious it was, then, for Jacob to bless Pharaoh! It would have been an insufferably arrogant act, unless it came from a man who remembered the Lord's promise to his grandfather, Abraham, to bless all families of the earth through him (Gen. 12:1–3). God had blessed Jacob so that he could be a blessing to the nations. So when Jacob met Pharaoh, he pronounced a benediction upon him by faith. Jacob understood that he had something valuable to give to mighty Pharaoh: the blessing of God Almighty.

Ultimately, that blessing for all nations is to be found in the person of Jesus Christ, the true son of Abraham. Whatever else we may or may not have to give to people around us, the greatest treasure we possess is Jesus. The greatest blessing we can pass on to our friends, to our families, and to our children is Jesus Christ. Jesus experienced the pain and suffering that goes with every sojourn here on earth. The days of his earthly sojourn were far shorter than Jacob's—less than even half of the biblical norm for a lifetime, seventy years. Those few days were filled with profound suffering and pain; he was well acquainted with sickness and sorrow, with mourning for dead friends, with betrayal and abandonment by his disciples, and finally with profound separation from his beloved Father on the cross. If anyone ever had the right to characterize the days of the years of his sojourn as nasty, brutish, and short, it was Jesus. Yet we see none of Jacob's bitterness in Jesus, but rather a constant spirit of thankfulness for his Father's good gifts, submission to the bitter aspects of his Father's will, and forgiveness for those who sinned against him. He took these great and lasting afflictions upon himself for us, so that we, his family, might receive the blessing that we had forfeited through our sin and might enjoy life beyond this life, a true home at the end of our earthly sojourn. He also took these sufferings upon himself for the joy that was set before him, for the joy of winning back a people to become God's special possession in him (Heb. 12:2). Through Christ, God's mercy now rests on aliens and strangers from all nations, as they come to God and receive in him eternal rest for their souls.

In Christ, you do not get what you deserve. Instead, what you get is something so amazing that you could never deserve it: God's overwhelming grace. This grace takes your pain and suffering and weaves it into part of God's glorious redemptive purpose. Your sins are nailed to the cross with Jesus, so that you don't have to fear their consequences anymore, and Christ's perfect righteousness is given to you, so that you now receive the Father's favor, earned by the Son through his obedient suffering. This grace now opens wide the way to our heavenly home and assures us that whatever the circumstances of our earthly sojourn, good or evil, there is a glorious inheritance stored up for us, which thieves cannot steal and moths cannot destroy, and from which no power in heaven or on earth or under the earth can separate us. Our blessing is a promised inheritance that is kept safe for us by God, a true home where glory waits for us in the arms of Jesus.

FOR FURTHER REFLECTION

1. How was Jacob's assessment of his life wrong? How was it accurate?
2. How did God treat Jacob, Joseph, and his brothers better than they deserved?
3. How has God treated you better than you have deserved?
4. What of your just desserts have fallen on Jesus instead of you? What of Jesus' just desserts do you enjoy now? What of his just desserts will you enjoy in the future?

CHAPTER TWELVE

FAMOUS LAST WORDS (GENESIS 47:28–48:22)

There is a reason why people record the last words of the dying. Sometimes, of course, those last sayings are not particularly profound, as when Humphrey Bogart concluded his life with the words, "I should never have switched from scotch to martinis." Yet often the process of dying concentrates the mind on the things that are most important, especially when that dying process is lengthy and protracted. Dying often strips away pretense and hypocrisy and lays bare the truth about a person's soul. It was interesting, therefore, to read the atheist Christopher Hitchens's final article before he died after a long struggle with cancer. In characteristically witty and thoughtful style, Hitchens explored the foolishness of Nietzsche's saying, "Whatever does not kill me only makes me stronger," concluding instead that there is much in this world that may not kill us, but certainly makes us weaker than it found us, including many modern cancer treatments.[1]

In Genesis 48 and 49, we have Jacob's last words. In contrast to Hitchens's firm belief to the end that this life is all that there is, Jacob's final testament is full of faith and hope in the God who had a purpose for his life before he was born and was not finished with his life when he died. The contrast between the two reflections is stark: one believed that there is no God, but that you should go ahead and enjoy your life anyway, while the other saw his whole life defined by his relationship to God—whether pursuing him, running away from him, or wrestling with him. Hitchens believed that life has no meaning beyond what we invest it with, that death is the end, and that beyond it is nothing. Jacob looked forward to God fulfilling his promises to him and to his offspring after him for generations to come. This passage challenges each of us also to ponder what we believe about life—and about the way in which we will think about our own mortality when death inevitably comes.

A DEATHBED BLESSING

Genesis 48 opens with Joseph bringing his two sons to the elderly, nearly blind Jacob to be blessed. This scene recalls the time when Jacob came to receive a blessing from his own elderly, visually impaired father (Gen. 27). On that occasion, Isaac tried to keep the ceremony a secret in order to bless his favorite son, Esau, instead of Jacob, in spite of God's oracle in favor of Jacob prior to his birth. This time, even though another reversal would occur, both sons were brought to be blessed openly, without deception or trickery. While Esau was excluded, both of Joseph's sons received a blessing, as would the rest of Joseph's brothers in Genesis 49. The line of God's promise was now branching out into a tree, as the blessed family became a harmonious community of peoples (48:4).

When Jacob heard that Joseph had arrived, he summoned his strength and sat up to deliver his profound final reflection. Perhaps triggered by the thought of the similarity of this moment to the episode in his youth, he began by reflecting on his own life. He recalled the experience of leaving and returning to Canaan, an experience bracketed by two key events (Gen. 48:3–7). When he left his homeland with nothing, he received God's promise of blessing at Luz (later known as Bethel; Gen. 28). Then, on his return to the Promised Land twenty years later, his beloved Rachel died and was buried in Canaan, on the road to Bethlehem.

These two events represent Jacob's life as a whole, which from beginning to end was lived in the tension between God's wonderful promise and the bitter reality of life's pain and struggle. God promised Jacob at the beginning of his life's journey the blessing originally given to Abraham, that he would become a mighty and harmonious people, receiving the land of Canaañ as an everlasting possession. Yet during his own lifetime, Jacob himself did not see anything remotely close to the fulfillment of that promise. He first received the promise while leaving the land, running for his life; and when he returned to Canaan, that return was marked, not by triumphal entry into his promised inheritance, but by an experience of the deepest pain and loss possible, the death of a beloved spouse.

It is therefore a mark of Jacob's profound faith that at the end of his life he wished to pass this blessing on to his grandchildren. Though he had not seen it fulfilled himself, Jacob still believed passionately that the promised blessing mattered and was worth passing on. Even Jacob's experience of devastating loss at Ephrath became a testament to his faith in God. Rachel's dying wish was to call her newborn boy Ben-oni ("son of my affliction"). Instead, Jacob named him Benjamin ("son of my right hand"), proclaiming his confidence that God would transform the painful circumstances of Benjamin's birth into a blessing, bringing something beautiful out of his deep suffering. The same faith shaped Joseph's thinking as well, as the name of one of the boys now in front of Jacob testified. Joseph named him Ephraim ("fruitful"), because "God has made me fruitful in the land of my affliction" (Gen. 41:52).

Jacob and Joseph were united in their faith, born out of hard experience, that God could turn sorrowful affliction into fruitful blessing.

Perhaps you find yourself in the midst of some bitter disappointment and loss right now. It could be a relationship that has been shattered, or severe health challenges, or the loss of someone you love dearly. Tears and suffering are often part of our earthly pilgrimage, just as they were for Jacob and Joseph. Yet the sovereign God we serve is able to bring fruit out of those sufferings. He is able to turn the offspring born out of the bitter experience of affliction into the most precious and profound markers of his closeness to us, as he walks alongside us through the deepest darkness.

THE PROMISE OF LAND

In spite of the challenges and painful disappointments of his life, Jacob's faith in God's promise of land and family runs like a golden thread throughout this chapter. First, there is the promise of land. It is not coincidental that both of the key events of Jacob's life that he remembers took place "in the land of Canaan" (Gen. 48:3, 7). Nor was it a random impulse that led Jacob to give Joseph the one piece of the Promised Land that he had conquered himself, a ridge of land that he took from the Amorites with his sword and bow (48:22). That was a remarkable bequest, given that Joseph was the second-in-command in Egypt and had abundant possessions there. What did he need with a small parcel of land in faraway Canaan? Wasn't that about as useful as the hideous, hand-knitted sweater that your great-aunt insists on giving you at Christmas? That gift was a symbol of Jacob's firm faith that God would one day bring Joseph's descendants back to the land of their fathers, and that a time would come when that property would become a valuable inheritance.

Given the focus of these blessings on the promise of land, it would be better to translate Jacob's blessing on Ephraim and Manasseh in verse 16 as "let them grow into a multitude in the midst of the *land*" rather than "in the midst of the *earth*." The Hebrew word *'erets* can mean either "land" or "earth," which leads to confusion elsewhere in the Bible. In the Beatitudes, for example, almost all English translations have Jesus saying, "Blessed are the meek, for they shall inherit the earth" (Matt. 5:5). Yet Jesus is quoting Psalm 37:11, where the same translations rightly render it, "The meek shall inherit the land and delight themselves in abundant peace." What difference does the translation make? The answer is that you don't need any spiritual interest to desire to inherit the earth. You can inherit the earth while living in Egypt as easily as in Canaan. Inheriting the land, however, involves meekly receiving the portion that the Lord has marked out for you, whether it is large or small, easy or challenging. Jacob was not asking that Joseph's sons should necessarily become great, as the world reckons greatness; rather, he wanted God to make them great in the Promised Land, the place where the Lord had chosen to place his name.

That distinction provides a helpful yardstick for our own hopes and dreams. Do you long to grow great in the earth—to be the kind of person that everyone around you envies because you have it all: career, influence, the perfect family, uninterrupted health? Or rather, is your heart's desire to grow great in the land, to seek the spiritual blessings found in God's kingdom alone? In the Sermon on the Mount, Jesus says that kingdom greatness is very different from worldly greatness. Kingdom greatness means being content with poverty, servanthood, and cross-bearing, as our lives are increasingly conformed to the cruciform pattern of Christ's life. Kingdom greatness means growing in meekness, not in self-assertiveness. It means learning how to mourn and to move toward those in pain, rather than how to evade suffering for ourselves and in the lives of others. It means loving and pursuing peace, which often feels far more costly than seeking to get our own way. Kingdom greatness will sometimes mean being persecuted, abandoned, and betrayed by those around us, yet finding that God is still our refuge. That is the kind of greatness that Jacob asks for Ephraim and Manasseh, and it is the kind of greatness that Jesus calls us to seek. Of course, none of us naturally desires such greatness. Much of the long, hard slog of discipleship involves God's retraining of our appetites away from the superficial things of this world toward the lasting treasures found only in him.

THE PROMISE OF FAMILY

Alongside the Lord's promise of land was the promise of family. Jacob poignantly said to Joseph, "I never expected to see your face again, and now God has allowed me to see your children too" (Gen. 48:11 NIV). The apparent loss of Joseph was one of the most painful and difficult challenges of Jacob's life, yet in the end the Lord not only restored Joseph to him, but enabled him to see Joseph's children as well. What a transformation from sorrow to joy! But Jacob's words were not just the joy of a happy grandfather. Literally, he called Joseph's boys his "seed," alluding to God's promise of blessing on Abraham's seed, and behind it to God's promise to send a seed of the woman, who would crush the head of the serpent and thus restore mankind to fellowship with God (Gen. 3:15). The promise to Abraham of numerous offspring was now passed on to the next generation, as Jacob asked God that Joseph's sons might become a multitude (48:16).

Indeed, although both sons were to be blessed with many offspring, the greater blessing was given to the younger brother, Ephraim, rather than to the oldest, Manasseh. God once again reversed the natural order of things. Ephraim would become a multitude of nations. This was another part of God's promise that Jacob had barely begun to see fulfilled. The family that went down to Egypt was a mere seventy people, a drop in the teeming bucket of Egypt's population. They could easily have been lost without a trace, assimilated into the wider Egyptian population. Yet, by faith, Jacob anticipated and prayed for what the first hearers of this story could see with their own eyes: the vast multitude of his descendants that emerged from Egypt under Moses some four hundred years later.

Undergirding these promises of land and offspring was the character of Jacob's God, which is the central piece of Jacob's testament in this chapter. We commented earlier on the pessimistic nature of Jacob's testimony before Pharaoh on his arrival in Egypt: "Few and evil have been the days of the years of my life, and they have not attained to the days of the years of the life of my fathers in the days of their sojourning" (Gen. 47:9). Here, however, following seventeen peaceful years with Joseph by his side, he is able to give a more balanced assessment of his life. To be sure, his life had been indelibly marked by pain and sorrow, marks that were prominent in this reflection. Rachel's death and the loss of Joseph were just two of the hard experiences that clamor to be remembered. Yet with the greater perspective of those last happy years in Egypt, Jacob could see and testify to what God had been doing throughout his life. So in Genesis 48:15–16, Jacob described the Lord as "the God before whom my fathers Abraham and Isaac walked, the God who has been my shepherd all my life long to this day, the angel who has redeemed me from all evil." Here Jacob highlighted two aspects of God's character: he is faithful, and he is the shepherd who redeems his people from all evil.

THE FAITHFUL GOD

First, Jacob's God is faithful. The Lord was the God of his father and of his grandfather before him, the God of Abraham and Isaac. He would be the God of his son and his grandsons after him as well: the God of Joseph, the God of Ephraim and Manasseh, as well as the God of their descendants down to the present day. This is a precious truth. In the Bible, God doesn't come to people as random, unconnected individuals; he deals with them as families. Many of us are also witness to that fact. We were not the first in our family to believe in Christ: our parents believed before us and, in some cases, their parents before them for generations. In other cases, you may be the first of your family to trust in God. Even so, you are not saved alone. God makes a promise not just to be your God, but to be the God of your children also, drawing them also to himself through faith in Christ.

This is the logic behind the baptism of covenant children. If God dealt with us as individuals who were left to make our own personal decision whether to follow him or not, then baptizing babies would make no sense. It would make sense for us only to baptize adults at the point at which they profess personal faith in Christ. But Abraham did not wait until Isaac was an adult to circumcise him; he was commanded to circumcise him on the eighth day as a mark of the Lord's sovereign choice to be Isaac's God (Gen. 17:10–14). Isaac did the same thing to Jacob, remembering God's call on Jacob's life before he was even born. He realized that what was of primary importance was God's choice, not Jacob's choice. Of course, circumcision was not an automatic guarantee of blessing, any more than baptism is. Ishmael and Esau were physically circumcised, but as they grew up it became clear that their hearts had not been renewed by God. They had the form of the blessing, but not the reality.

The circumcision of children in the Old Testament was thus never a testimony about a person's choice of the Lord to be their God; it was always an act of wondering faith on the part of the parent that the Lord was willing to be the God of their children also. How amazing it is that the holy God, who created the universe, is willing to be our children's God too! When we baptize our children, we declare that the promise of God on the day of Pentecost is still true: the Lord promised to give his Holy Spirit to us and to our children—as well as to many who are still afar off, who do not come from Christian homes and families, but who, by God's incredible grace, will be incorporated into his family as adults (Acts 2:38–39). Our God is faithful to us and to our children, and promises to give the gift of faith in Christ to all those whom he has chosen and called.

This faithfulness of God is intensely precious to all of us who know ourselves to be dysfunctional parents. We sin daily against our children by loving them too little and by loving them too much. Sometimes we expose them thoughtlessly to dangerous situations, while in others we shelter them destructively from difficult experiences that would make them stronger. Instead of consistently speaking the gospel to them, we impose our arbitrary personal laws upon them. Our own lives are inconsistent examples of holiness at best, and much of the time, instead of passing on the fear of the Lord, we hand down to them the oppressive idols that we ourselves worship as parents. What hope do our poor children have of growing up to love God?

The answer that we proclaim to our children in baptism is that they have exactly the same hope that we have, which rests in the unchanging faithfulness of God. The gospel of God's mercy is as true for them as it is for us. They can be saved in spite of all of their weakness, brokenness, and sin, just as we are, through God's overpowering grace. The God who loves our children far more than we do can adopt them just as they are, full of the brokenness that they have inherited from us and the new patterns of brokenness that they are developing on their own. Our

God takes whole families of broken, sinful people and redeems them in Christ.

THE SHEPHERD WHO REDEEMS US FROM EVIL

The second truth that Jacob declares in his testament is that God is the shepherd who redeems him from evil (Gen. 48:15–16). That is a remarkable claim because of the breadth of the Hebrew word translated here "evil" (*ra‘*). It encompasses not only moral evil, but also what we might call "situational evil": both the bad things that are done to us and the bad things that just seem to happen to us. That is why this word is sometimes rendered elsewhere as "harm" (e.g., in 31:29). Yet can it really be said that Jacob's God protected him from all harm, so that none of the bad things that typically happen to people in this broken world happened to him?

Clearly, that cannot be what Jacob was saying. He had already mentioned the pain of losing a beloved spouse and the agony of those twenty years when he thought Joseph was dead. His life had been filled with painful experiences that came through the circumstances of his life and through the deliberate sins of others against him. What Jacob was affirming was that his God had *redeemed* all of that evil. It is not that bad things never happened to him, but rather that those bad things were worked by God into something that was good. In fact, the Hebrew word for "redeem" (*ga'al*) presupposes that something evil has been transcended by a greater act of good. This word is used for rescuing someone who has lost everything and has had to sell his property, whether through incompetence or misfortune; his redeemer is a relative who has the responsibility to buy back his inheritance (Lev. 25:25). Sometimes people became so desperate that they sold themselves into slavery: their redeemer was a kinsman who, at his own expense, bought them back and restored their freedom (Lev. 25:47–49).

This is what Jacob was affirming about God. He had redeemed all of the tragic events of Jacob's life. Instead of destroying him, these traumatic experiences had been so redeemed by God that now good flowed from them instead. None of Jacob's pain had been wasted. None of his sorrow had been fruitless wandering in the wilderness. Throughout all the days of his life, the good shepherd had been leading him along the right pathways, whether to green pastures or through the valley of deep shadow, providing good for him and redeeming evil, bringing blessing and hope out of the darkest and most desperate situations (cf. Ps. 23).

It is striking to note that only an old person can bear this kind of testimony to God's faithfulness and power to redeem evil. When Jacob left his home so many years earlier, he might have affirmed these truths theoretically, but it was only at the end of his life that he could affirm them experientially. Young people may have great energy and enthusiasm, but they often need to sit and learn at the feet of those who, by long, hard, and sometimes bitter experience, have come to know more deeply the character of our faithful Lord and Shepherd.

JESUS, OUR REDEEMER

Now the days of Jacob's sojourn here on earth were almost over. But before he left, he wanted to pass on the blessing of this faithful, shepherding, redeeming God to his children. The same blessing belongs also to us, since we are the spiritual descendants of Jacob, members of the Israel of God (Gal. 6:16). We can see and testify even more fully than Jacob that the Lord is our faithful shepherd, who redeems our evil. From where we stand, we see the enormity of what it truly cost God to become our Redeemer.

In order to become our kinsman who redeems us, God's own Son had to leave the eternal smile of his Father's blessing and enter this world of suffering and evil. Jesus

Christ had to expose himself to the hatred and enmity that this world has for whatever is good and holy, and to learn through harsh experience how to trust his Father in the dark times as well as the good times. Jesus received a body that could experience evil in its most vicious forms. He had a back that could be scourged and beaten until it was bloody and raw, hands and feet of living flesh that could be pierced by cruel nails, a side that could be stabbed with a spear, and a heart that could be broken by hypocrisy, treachery, ingratitude, faithlessness, and abandonment. The one who is himself the Good Shepherd took the place of his errant sheep in order to rescue us from the dangers of the valley of death's deep shadow. The faithful Son was abandoned by his own Father in order to buy us back from our bondage and return to us the inheritance that we squandered through our own sin and evil. He redeemed us from all evil by taking upon himself the punishment that our sin deserves as its penalty and by covering us with his perfect holiness and purity. That is the power of the cross: the Son of God who was slain for us now clothes us with his perfect righteousness, thereby accomplishing God's eternal purpose to have a holy people who would belong to him forever.

Do you see the power of Jacob's last testament? Here was a man who was ready to die because he understood the true meaning of his life and knew personally the one who had promised to be with him in life and in death. The shepherd who had walked with him all the days of his life would not abandon him, now that he was dying. The redeemer who had purchased him from his bondage to sin and death would not give up ownership of his soul to the last enemy, death itself. The promise that God gave him in his youth was always deeper and richer than giving Jacob a people and a land. It was a promise to be Jacob's guide until death and his God forever (Ps. 48:14). God undertook to prepare a feast for Jacob and to welcome him to dwell in his house forever (Ps. 23:6).

We are all dying. None of us knows how long we have to live or when God will call us to meet him. Are you ready to meet this God, as Jacob was? Do you have a similar testimony that God is your shepherd and redeemer? Perhaps today is the day that he is calling you to enter into a new relationship with him, as your shepherd and king. Submit your heart today to his sovereign call and bow before him in faith, looking to what Christ has done as your righteousness and hope.

If you are already trusting in this God, remember today that he is your faithful shepherd, who will redeem all of your evil. That means that all of the evil circumstances in your life right now—the sins that others are committing against you, or the sins you have committed that are bearing bitter fruit, or those out-of-control aspects of your life that are so painful—are under his sovereign control and will not be wasted. Yes, they really are evil. You don't have to pretend that these events are something other than that. We live in an evil and broken world. However, as the cross and the resurrection of Jesus demonstrate, we serve a God who regularly brings glorious light out of the deepest darkness, beautiful good out of the ugliest evil, perfect healing out of painful sickness, and resurrection life out of death itself. This is the faithful, shepherding God who has committed himself to lead you until the day of your death and then welcome you into a glorious inheritance in Christ, in which all of the evil of your life will be beautifully and wondrously redeemed.

FOR FURTHER REFLECTION

1. How did Jacob's last words reflect both the reality of his suffering and his hope in God's promise?
2. Jacob passed on the promises of land and seed. Are these promises still relevant for us today? How?

3. How has God demonstrated his faithfulness to you and your family? What part of his work in and through families is most encouraging to you in your present stage of life?

4. What is the relationship between evil and redemption? How did God redeem Jacob's suffering?

5. Jesus is our kinsman-redeemer, who acted on our behalf at great cost to himself. How has he redeemed you from evil in your life?

CHAPTER THIRTEEN

MIXED BLESSINGS
(GENESIS 49:1–28)

Where are true happiness and blessing to be found? Well, where are you looking for them? One way to discover the answer to that question is to look at the New Year's resolutions that you've made. Whether they are carefully inscribed in the first page of your diary or fleeting desires to stop doing the stupid things that mess up your life, it is revealing to ponder what your resolutions say about your hopes and dreams and thus your sense of where blessing is to be found. Perhaps your desire is to get organized, or stop dating losers, or lose twenty pounds, or spend more time with your children. Whatever your resolution, it is worth asking what would be different in your life if you attained your goal. After all, we generally long for good things. Nobody resolves to start dating losers, to gain fifty pounds, to eat more junk food, or to lose their keys more often. But are these really the things in which true blessing is to be found? So much of what we long for is merely trivial, or at best a substitute for what is really important in life, our relationship with God. It is in knowing God through Jesus Christ that true blessing is to be found.

A BOOK ABOUT BLESSING

The book of Genesis is a book about blessing. When God created the world, he blessed it (Gen. 1:22, 28). In the beginning, the perfect universe existed under the smile of its perfect Creator. Yet that universal blessing was lost through the sin of the first couple, Adam and Eve. The fruitful, safe, and peaceful world that they had been given was now filled with thorns and thistles, interpersonal conflict, bodily pains, and ultimately death, by which their bodies returned to the dust. Worst of all, the perfect relationship with God that they experienced in the garden of Eden was lost as they were driven out of God's presence into the cold and dark reality that we all now experience. Blessing turned to curse.

Yet from the beginning the Lord our God has been determined to deliver us from all of our evil and to turn our self-imposed curse into restored blessing. In large measure, the book of Genesis is the story of that restored blessing, promised and partially received. The Lord promised that the seed of the woman would crush the head of the serpent, restoring the relationship that sin had broken (Gen. 3:15). Yet that restorative work would not be short or painless. Far from redeeming humanity, the first "seed of the woman," Cain, took sin to the next level by murdering his own brother (Gen. 4). That downward spiral of sin continued in the subsequent generations until, at the time of the flood, every thought of mankind was only evil, all of the time (6:5). Even after the flood, sin continued to rear its ugly head. The same self-confidence and independent spirit that caused the first sin culminated in the building of the Tower of Babel, an arrogant assertion that by working together and using technological skill, mankind could force its way back into God's presence (11:1–9). Far from assuring blessing for its builders, however, the tower resulted in further curse and the scattering of humanity.

These stories show us that a new beginning of blessing could never come from human initiative. It would need to come from God, and that redeeming plan began at the end of Genesis 11 when God called Abram and Sarai, promising to bless them and make them a blessing for the whole world. The rest of Genesis is the partial outworking of that promised blessing in the lives of four generations of broken, sinful people.

That is the wider context for the blessings in Genesis 49. Jacob is pronouncing God's word to each of his children, a process that started with the double blessing for Joseph's two children, Ephraim and Manasseh. Now Jacob gathered all twelve of his children to give a final word of blessing to each. The news was not all good. Some of the "blessings" don't seem much like blessings at all. In some cases, judgment for the sins of the parents will fall also on their children. But the keynote of Jacob's speech is still blessing, as verse 28 makes clear, for all of his sons are included in the foundational blessing of being part of God's people. Unlike Abraham and Isaac, Jacob would not see any of his sons cut off from the promise. All twelve were included in God's plan, in spite of their sin. Certainly, they were not better people than Esau or Ishmael, as Jacob's words make clear. It was simply God's purpose and plan to show grace and favor to the whole of what would later become the nation of Israel. Yet the shape of these blessings highlights a number of key themes in God's relationship with his people.

THE ONGOING REALITY OF SIN

First, these blessings show us the ongoing reality and consequences of sin in the life of God's people. It is not just unbelievers who exhibit deep-rooted and ongoing patterns of sin, but believers as well. This is evident in Jacob's words to several of the brothers, starting with the oldest. As the firstborn, Reuben had pride of place, humanly speaking: he had strength, might, honor, and power. Yet all of that opportunity and potential was wasted because he was as solid and dependable as water (Gen. 49:4). His character was first revealed in the incident where he lay with his father's concubine, Bilhah, in an attempt to seize control of the family (35:22). In the Joseph story, Reuben was the one whose plans never quite worked out. He planned to rescue Joseph from the pit, but he was gone at the crucial moment when the other brothers sold him into slavery (37:29–30). Reuben later proposed using the life of his two sons as surety that Benjamin would return from the trip to Egypt, but his callous offer was rejected by his father (42:37–38). That's the story of Reuben's life: circumstances and his own character seemed continually to conspire against him. That trait of unreliability was also passed on to the tribe that came from him (see Judg. 5:15–16).

Next in line, Simeon and Levi revealed themselves to be violent and ruthless men when, after the rape of Dinah, they tricked the men of Shechem into being circumcised in order to massacre them (Gen. 49:5–6; see ch. 34). At the time, Jacob took no action, but the lasting result of their sin was that their descendants would be scattered throughout Israel. As Simeon and Levi were joined together in their iniquity, so the tribes that came from them would together be scattered in their judgment.

Then there are Zebulun and Issachar. Zebulun would end up living by the seashore, a little too close to the pagan town of Sidon, in pursuit of the advantages of trade that such a location offered. Issachar's pursuit of a comfortable situation in life would also succeed, but the end result would be that their descendants would be put under forced labor (Gen. 49:13–15). It seems that the earthly lot of both tribes would be materially pleasant, but their blessing implies that there would be a cost to seeking their treasure in this world. Did they ever ask whether their earthly success was worth the price that they paid? Or did they sell their souls, like so many others, not for the whole world, but merely for the prospect of a comfortable and easy life?

We could add to that list of dubious blessings, though not all of them are equally clear. Benjamin, the baby of the family, is a ravenous wolf—never a positive picture in Scripture (Gen. 49:27). Morning and evening, he carves up the spoil from those weaker than himself. Dan is a serpent along the way (49:17). Asher produces rich delicacies, fit for royalty, while Naphtali is as wild as a mountain deer (49:20–21).

These blessings show us the complexity of sin. Sin can be socially reprehensible, as when it involves sleeping with your father's concubine or massacring a city. Alternatively, it can be socially lauded, as in pursuing a good living by providing rich delicacies for foreigners at the cost of your spiritual distinctiveness. What is more, this passage reminds us that sin often has multigenerational consequences. These blessings were not just for the patriarchs themselves; they were also for their children and their children's children, who were all in some way affected by the sins of their parents.

The same is true of our own sin. There are some sins that we easily identify because they are widely regarded as socially reprehensible. Drunkenness, murder, and child abuse are generally recognized as wrong, even by the often-warped standards of modern society. Yet other sins are not so easily identified, because they have come to be regarded as neutral or even virtuous in our society. Sexual promiscuity has become the new normal, to the point where lifelong abstinence or marital fidelity are seen as somehow odd. Pride and self-love are strongly inculcated into us from our earliest days. There are magazines whose entire purpose is gossip, yet they are not hidden on the top shelf of the store in plain wrappers. When Paul told the Ephesians, "Let there be no filthiness nor foolish talk nor crude joking, which are out of place, but instead let there be thanksgiving" (Eph. 5:4), he was not only out of step with ancient Ephesian culture, but with our culture too. "Filthiness" and "crude joking" are an apt description of a large part of our culture of entertainment and of much of our regular conversation, even within the Christian community. How many of us have even considered the possibility that devoting our lives to comfort and material success might leave us enslaved to sinful compromise? We are all Reubens, Simeons, Levis, and Zebuluns.

Do we think about the impact that our sins have on others around us—our friends, our spouses, and especially our children? The effects on the family of pornography, adultery, drunkenness, and abuse are clear, but what about more subtly corrosive patterns of behavior? One painful lesson I learned from my family was that I never quite measured up to their expectations. I was never the favorite, and I never felt that I was quite approved. That deep hurt now bears bitter fruit in all kinds of sinful responses in my own heart and my relationships, as I constantly strive to win the approval of others and of God and to prove to everyone that I really can be successful. Some of the behaviors that emerge from that inner darkness are things that people easily recognize as unlovely and unattractive; from it flows an arrogant attitude centered on myself that rarely celebrates the successes of others. It appears in a caustic tongue that uses wit to raise myself up by putting others down. However, there are other fruits of my heart idolatry that our society applauds and praises, such as my relentless drive to work hard and succeed. People generally regard it as a good thing that I am up at 5 a.m. working on writing projects, even though that restlessness is often driven by sinful fears and desires. These specific sins with which I struggle impact my own children as well. If I find it hard to measure up to my own expectations, how hard are they going to find it to do so? In the same way, perhaps you also struggle with deep-rooted family patterns of sin and with idolatries that you learned from your parents.

PATTERNS OF SIN REDEEMED

Although sin has multigenerational consequences, they are not inevitable and irredeemable, as the Levites demonstrated. By the grace of God, their curse of being dispersed among the nation was transformed into a blessing, for they received the privilege of becoming the priestly tribe (Deut. 33:8–11). The Levites still had no earthly inheritance of their own, but the Lord himself became their inheritance. They were scattered throughout Israel and Judah in order to bring the blessing of instruction in God's law to the people wherever they were. The consequences of their father's curse became the context in which they became a blessing to others. Their character trait of seeing things in black and white, which earlier led them into sin, was put to redeemed use in the Lord's service.

It is the same for us. You may have been deeply hurt and damaged by the sin of your parents or your family, but that brokenness does not define you. The wounds that you have suffered may be real and deep, and they may create tremendous struggles within you that will shape the rest of your life in significant ways. God doesn't promise to wave a magic wand and fix that pain, removing all of your struggles. Yet the story of the Levites shows that God can transform the effects of curse into an opportunity for blessing. He has the power to redeem our evil and bring good from it. Your weakness and brokenness may equip you to appreciate the gospel more deeply than would otherwise be the case. The struggles of your own personal history may enable you to minister to others in unique ways because of that particular experience of pain and loss. Many of the best counselors have struggled deeply with sin and brokenness in their own lives, which then equips them to help others with their struggles. God can use the trauma of your experiences for profound good in the lives of others.

Most importantly, notice that all of these sinners, along with their sin-damaged offspring, are incorporated into the line of promise. Israel is not built on the foundation of righteous Joseph, or even transformed Judah, but on the foundation of all twelve patriarchs. Unstable Reuben, violent Simeon and Levi, comfort-loving Issachar, and dangerous Benjamin are all included as part of God's saving purpose to have a holy people for himself. That is truly remarkable. Our redeeming God does not go searching through the world for the best and most faithful people to save; rather, he comes seeking and saving lost sinners like us. God pursues and rescues those whose lifestyles make them the object of the world's scorn, as well as those whose sin the world admires and lauds. From the start, our salvation has been entirely by God's incredible grace and not by our works. There is no room in this list of ancestors for any boasting or pride in human accomplishment. The work of saving us is God's from start to finish.

The profound lesson for us here is that the Bible takes our sin neither too lightly nor too seriously. On the one hand, sin is not trivial. The Bible lovingly warns of the bitter fruit that sin bears in our own lives and in the lives of others around us. Sin is destructive, though it poses as the way to true freedom and joy. Yet sin shall not have the last word in our destiny. Instead, the Bible encourages sinners to remember that those who are chosen and saved by God, through his grace alone, can never be disinherited. We may be broken in many different ways, but if we are joined to God's people through Christ, we can never be broken off and cast away. God's grace trumps all of our sin, and he will use our struggles with sin to bring about profound spiritual fruit in our lives, as through them we grow in patience, humility, and dependence upon God.

EVIL CIRCUMSTANCES REDEEMED

The second thing Jacob's blessings portray is the faithfulness of God in redeeming our evil circumstances. This theme from the blessing on Ephraim and Manasseh is reiterated here in the blessing on their father, Joseph. He received the richest blessing, as you might expect, given Jacob's special love for him. His blessing also reflected his life story. Joseph was abundantly fruitful, sending out branches from his well-watered vine, moving out beyond his own walled vineyard (Gen. 49:22). However, that prosperity came in the context of affliction and assault. Joseph was attacked by the archers (49:23), a reference to all of the slanders and injustices he had to endure throughout his lifetime. Yet the central word in this blessing is neither Joseph's native fruitfulness, nor his bitter affliction, but God's purposes in his life. Joseph's blessing flowed from the Mighty One of Jacob, who strengthened his arms— from the Shepherd who was with him, from the "Stone of Israel" (49:24).

The "Stone of Israel" here is probably not a title for God. Elsewhere, he is called the "Rock of Israel," but that is a quite different word.[1] Stones are often references to memorials raised by God's people to remind them of his faithfulness, like the one near Mizpah called Ebenezer ("stone of help" in 1 Samuel 7:12) or the stone pillar that Jacob raised at Bethel to symbolize God's promise to bless him (Gen. 28:18). The point is not to exalt Joseph's innate strength of character and his faithfulness to God. Rather, those qualities flowed from God's strengthening of Joseph and faithfulness to him. God set him apart from his brothers, and God maintained his faith in the face of every bitter assault.

That is why, even though Joseph had already achieved greatness in Egypt and possessed wealth, status, and power in abundance, Jacob still blessed him. The blessings that Joseph needed did not consist in things that Egypt could give. Rather, they were the same blessings that were first promised to Joseph's grandfather, Isaac, and to his great-grandfather, Abraham. Jacob blessed Joseph with the blessing of breast and womb, which represents fruitfulness in children, and the blessing of the everlasting hills, the blessing of land (Gen. 49:25–26). These were the twin blessings that God first promised Abraham. Jacob's blessing on Joseph reiterated his blessing on Ephraim and Manasseh, that they would become great in the land of promise, receiving the fullness of what God had promised to Abraham (48:16).

Even though the longest and richest blessing was reserved for Joseph, the blessing on Judah was the most remarkable. Jacob blessed Judah with the same exaltation that Joseph saw in his boyhood dream. In the days to come, his father's sons would come and bow down to Judah (Gen. 49:8). He is described in distinctly royal terms: majestic and lionlike, he will triumph over his enemies (49:9). He will possess the scepter and the ruler's staff (49:10), and his brothers will praise him (49:8). This blessing obviously foreshadowed the future history of Israel, in which the tribe of Judah would become the royal tribe, from which would come the line of David. Yet the prophecy also anticipated something even greater than the substantial blessings experienced by Judah in the time of David and Solomon. After all, the scepter first arrived in Judah in the time of David and Solomon, and verse 10 anticipates the scepter continuing with Judah until some greater, future arrival. Most ancient and modern translations have understood this verse as a messianic prophecy, rendering it, "until he comes to whom it [the scepter] belongs." This messianic interpretation is already clear in later biblical passages that allude to this verse.

This enigmatic "one to come," to whom rulership properly belongs, will not simply reign over the nation of Israel (Judah's brothers). His reign will extend more widely still, for the obedience of the nations is his (Gen. 49:10). He will be unmatched in beauty (49:12), and his coming will be marked by unparalleled prosperity. He will hitch his donkey to a choice vine (49:11), which would be rather like using one hundred dollar bills to light fires, since the donkey would immediately start munching the grapes, as well as the branches of the vine. Instead of washing his clothing in water, like ordinary people, this future king will be so rich that he can use wine for that purpose. Behind these images of tremendous prosperity and blessing, there are also ominous images of power: the wine is described as "the blood of grapes," and cleaning garments with wine would inevitably stain them red. Alongside a promise of prosperity for his people, this image shouts a clear warning of danger to all of the Messiah's enemies.

How much did Jacob understand of the distant future he foretold? We don't know. Certainly future generations wrestled with the meaning of this prophecy. Zechariah spoke hopefully of a future king who would come riding on the foal of a donkey to bring salvation and blessing to his people (Zech. 9:9-10). Yet none of the Davidic kings or their successors ever lived up to this role, before or after the Exile. Because of their sins, they were unable to establish the kind of peace and prosperity that the Lord had promised. If blessing was ever to come to such a weak people, sharing all of the brokenness that Judah himself demonstrated in Genesis 38, the Lord himself would have to be their redeemer. In Isaiah 63, we see the Lord coming from the east, from Bozrah in Edom, with his garments stained red with blood like someone trampling grapes. The Lord would act to bring salvation to his people and judgment upon their enemies, to redeem all those who belong to him and establish true righteousness and lasting peace (Isa. 63:1-7).

All of these images point us forward to Christ, the true Lion of the tribe of Judah (Rev. 5:5). He is the one to whom judgment and rulership truly belong, the one who came to earth to redeem his people. That is why Jesus turned water into abundant wine at Cana in his first miracle, using jars that were meant for washing (John 2). That is why Jesus rode into Jerusalem on a colt, the foal of a donkey, as the humble yet powerful king who saves his people (Matt. 21:1-8). Jesus is the promised one of unmatched beauty to whom the obedience of the nations belongs. Jesus is depicted in the book of Revelation riding on a white horse, wearing a robe dipped in blood, in order to tread the winepress of the fury of the wrath of God Almighty by defeating and judging all of his foes. He is the King of kings and Lord of lords (Rev. 19:11–16).

Yet Jesus did not need to come to earth and be born of Judah's line in order to be the powerful king who judges his enemies and crushes those who oppose him. The obedience of the nations belongs to him by rights as their God and Creator. Jesus did not need to be born in a stable and laid in a manger in order to wear a robe stained with his enemies' blood. He is the Almighty God, the first and the last, apart from whom there is no other (Rev. 1:17–18; Isa. 44:6). Jesus only needed to enter our world in order to be our redeemer, the one who turns our deserved curse into undeserved blessing. In order to rescue us from our lostness, God himself had to take on flesh and stain his garments with his own precious blood at the cross. He took up our affliction, so that we could now wash our sin-stained garments, not in blood-red wine, but in the blood of the Lamb himself (Rev. 7:14). As we wash our garments in his cleansing blood, they come out dazzlingly clean and white, as pure and spotless as if we had never sinned. He is the fulfillment of all that Jacob saw and more besides.

WAITING WITH HOPE

So how should you respond in the midst of the disappointments and trials of life, surrounded by people who constantly sin against you and seem unable to live up to their potential? How should you react when you recognize that you yourself constantly sin and fail to be the person you ought to be? Where is true blessing to be found for such messed-up people? Jacob models for us the right response in Genesis 49:18—he looked to the Lord, expressing an attitude of patient waiting for the Lord to complete his salvation. In some measure, Jacob had already experienced the Lord's deliverance. He praised God for it in Genesis 48:15–16. There were many ways in which God had answered his prayers and blessed him: he saw Joseph and his children, long after he thought that he would never behold his face again. But Jacob also knew that the blessings he had already seen were only a faint shadow of the salvation that was yet to come.

It is God's grace that enables us to wait with patience— patience with the brokenness around us and within us. It is grace that enables us not to take our sin too lightly or too heavily as we wait. Grace is the overarching theme of this chapter. By grace, all of Jacob's children receive the privilege of being numbered among God's people, receiving his blessing. They don't deserve it. They will continue to be undeserving, just like us. We too are unstable, violent, worldly, treacherous, compromised, and abusive—not exactly a description of the A-team. Yet God is determined to make us a holy nation, a kingdom of priests, a people belonging to him. It is not a position that you can forfeit by your inadequacies and transgressions, even though your sin may have very real consequences in your life. God's saints persevere to the end and receive his blessing, not because of their own intrinsic goodness and strength, but because of God's faithfulness and his commitment to bless them.

In due time, the Promised One will come again. Next time, Jesus will not come riding into Jerusalem humbly on a donkey; rather, he will come on the clouds in glorious triumph to consummate his marriage to his bride, the church. He will not come to bring blessing simply to the physical descendants of Jacob, but also to all those who are his spiritual heirs in faith. Are you waiting patiently for that return, looking with longing faith to Christ as your only hope of acceptance and blessing before God? As you and I trust in Christ, we become part of the redeemed community of God's people. We still wrestle with ongoing sin and its bitter fruit, but now we start to give Jesus the obedience that belongs to him, as the Holy Spirit works change in our hearts. In the face of the ugliness of our sin, we find comfort in the beauty of his holiness. As we endure difficult circumstances in life, we look forward to the fullness of his kingdom. We long for the day when his people from every tribe, nation, and language will gather around the throne, singing praises to the Lion of Judah, slain for them. In the meantime, as we wait for Christ's return, we are called to wait like Jacob, with patient, expectant hearts, looking to the Lord for our deliverance, confident that it will surely come and bring blessing with it.

FOR FURTHER REFLECTION

1. How would you define *blessing*? What is the significance of blessing in the Bible? How does Scripture define *blessing*?
2. Jacob's blessings highlight the ongoing reality of sin among God's people. What sins are easily identifiable in your life, your church, and your community? What sins are commonly tolerated or implicitly endorsed?
3. How did God redeem the consequences of sin in the tribes of Levi and Judah? How has God redeemed multigenerational sin in your church or community?
4. How did God extend blessing to Joseph in the midst of affliction? Has God given you experiences of blessing in the midst of suffering?
5. How do the mixed blessings given by Jacob relate to the blessings given by Jesus? How does Jesus fulfill the blessings pronounced on Judah? In what ways is that fulfillment surprising and unexpected?

CHAPTER FOURTEEN

DEAD AND BURIED?
(GENESIS 49:29–50:26)

Death, be not proud, though some have called thee
Mighty and dreadful, for thou art not so;
For those whom thou think'st thou dost overthrow,
Die not, poor Death, nor yet canst thou kill me.
One short sleep past, we wake eternally,
And death shall be no more; Death, thou shalt die.
—John Donne[1]

At the end of Hollywood movies, the heroes ride off into the sunset. At the end of biblical stories, the heroes die. The difference is not incidental. Hollywood has nothing better to offer than living happily ever after, glossing over the fact that no one lives forever. The biblical heroes, on the other hand, are men and women of faith, looking for a city that is not of this world. For them, a good death is a fitting end to a good life, not merely an unpleasant and unfortunate reality. Yes, death is the last enemy, but it is an enemy whose power is limited and who can be overcome, as John Donne so beautifully reflects in his sonnet. A good death is not a contradiction in terms, and this passage in the book of Genesis is about two good deaths, those of Jacob and Joseph. Yet this story is not simply about death; it is more precisely about death and burial. There is more to death than dying. Jacob and Joseph did not merely die well in the sense of dying comfortably at a good old age, surrounded by loving caregivers. They died well in the sense of dying in faith, knowing that their death was not the end of the real story of their lives. For Jacob and Joseph, the end of their life on earth was merely the closing page of one volume that leads on into a new and better sequel.

This is a profoundly relevant insight for all of us, for we will all die, unless the Lord returns first. Previous generations prepared people for the inevitable, while in our culture we hide from death, as if we could escape its power by denying its reality. In contrast, the Bible shows us how to overcome death's power by embracing its reality in the light of the greater power and purpose of the living God. In addition, sandwiched between the accounts of these two good deaths in Genesis is an important reminder that, in a broken and dysfunctional world, living well is sometimes also a great challenge. When our own sin results in significant evil, we struggle with guilt for our failures and shortcomings, which leads to fear and anxiety. Meanwhile, when the sin of others has evil consequences in our lives, we battle with resentment, which leads to anger and bitterness. How do you deal with guilt—your own guilt and the guilt that others incur—and break its power over you?

JACOB'S GOOD DEATH

Jacob lived to a ripe old age with his mind intact, even as his body failed. He was surrounded by his family, now at peace with one another. He saw his children's children and passed on his blessing. Now he was ready to go, after once more reiterating his instructions that he should be buried in the cave of Machpelah with Abraham, Isaac, and Sarah (Gen. 49:29–32). It is ironic that in death Jacob chose to lie with his unloved wife, Leah, as well as his grandfather and father, Abraham and Isaac, while his beloved Rachel lay buried elsewhere, on the road to Ephrath (Gen. 48:7). In antiquity, the decision to be buried in a particular place meant that you were permanently committing your body to a particular piece of ground, and therefore to the care of the god associated with it. Burial in the family inheritance (*achuzzah*) was Jacob's final act of faith in the promise of the Lord to be his God, as well as the God of his fathers. Thus far, the Lord had only given Jacob and his family possession of a tiny portion of the Promised Land. Yet he preferred to be buried there, rather than receive a state funeral in the land of Egypt.

It was a mark of Egypt's respect for Joseph and his father that the period of mourning for Jacob went on for seventy days (Gen. 50:3), only two less than that prescribed for the death of a pharaoh. When Joseph and his brothers returned to Canaan for Jacob's burial, they were accompanied by a large party of prominent Egyptians (50:7). Yet they followed a rather curious route. The normal road from Egypt to Canaan went up the Mediterranean coast and then cut inland, but this journey took them close to the River Jordan, to the east of the Promised Land (50:10). Apparently, the funeral procession went around the eastern side of the Dead Sea and had to cross the Jordan in order to enter the Promised Land. Commentaries suggest good political reasons why that route might have been required at that time, but the writer of Genesis is more interested in the theological resonances of this course. Jacob's corpse traversed the same route that his descendants would follow in their own exodus some four hundred years later.

This motif explains a number of other odd details in the account, such as the emphasis on "going up," which is an important verb in Exodus, as well as the mention of the children, flocks, and herds staying behind, as Pharaoh tried to insist on at the time of Moses. Perhaps most striking of all is the reference to the Egyptian chariots and horsemen.

187

In the Pentateuch, they are mentioned only here in Genesis 50:9 and in the account of the crossing of the Red Sea in Exodus 14 and 15. Chariots and horsemen may seem out of place at a funeral, but they would have a key part to play in the Exodus. All of these details show us that this last journey is Jacob's personal exodus out of Egypt, the initial fulfillment of God's promise that in the end he would bring Jacob back to the Promised Land (Gen. 46:3–4). Although the ultimate fulfillment would come in the later exodus of the whole people of Israel, the personal exodus of Jacob's corpse acted as a sign and guarantee of the later reality, the "firstfruits" of the promise (cf. 1 Cor. 15:20).

JOSEPH'S GOOD DEATH

Joseph also died a good death. He lived to the age of 110 years, which was considered the ideal in Egyptian literature, and he saw his children's children to the third generation (Gen. 50:22). Even though he lived in Egypt for ninety-three of his 110 years, it was not Joseph's home. When it came time to die, he gave instructions for his bones to be placed in a mobile grave as an act of faith, so that when Israel left Egypt he would be able to go with his people (50:25–26).

It is interesting to compare the differences in the burials of Jacob and Joseph. Why did Joseph not follow Jacob's example of being buried in Canaan straightaway? Perhaps Joseph was actually making an even stronger statement of his faith in God's purpose for Israel. Jacob's exodus was a personal event. It prefigured the great exodus of Israel and in a sense guaranteed it, but it did not depend on it. Jacob's body lay safely in the Promised Land, no matter what happened to his descendants. Joseph, however, tied his whole hope to that of his people. If Israel stayed in exile forever in Egypt, so would he. If God brought them up out of Egypt into the Promised Land, then his bones would go up with them. He staked his future resting place entirely on the fulfillment of God's promise for all of his people.

The fact that Joseph's burial gave testimony to God's promise is indicated by the box in which he was interred. Our English translations render the word as "coffin" (Gen. 50:26), though Biblical Hebrew has no term that exactly matches "coffin." The Israelites were not in the habit of putting people in a box; they simply wrapped the bodies and put them in a cave or in the ground. In fact, the Hebrew word used for Joseph's box is the same word that elsewhere refers to the ark of the covenant. In other words, all the way along their wilderness trail, the Israelites were actually carrying two arks, the ark of the covenant and the ark that contained Joseph's remains—both of which bore eloquent witness to the Lord's faithfulness to his people.

This is surely the note that should be sounded in a Christian funeral service. The dead are no longer with us, though their bodies remain. The conclusion to a good death is a gathering of God's people, not just to celebrate the person's life, but to celebrate our God and to declare our faith that his faithfulness to the deceased in life continues in death. We place the dead body in a box as a testimony to our faith and theirs of an exodus yet to come, when the final trumpet shall sound and the dead in Christ shall rise. Their souls will then be reunited to resurrected, glorified bodies, and we who remain alive when Christ returns shall be caught up with them to meet our returning King as he comes to judge the earth and establish his reign forever (1 Thess. 4:17). We plant that box in the ground like a seed, confident that the Lord of the harvest will, in due season, bring what is sowed in weakness to life in resurrection glory. We do so with confidence, because when Jesus rose from the dead and ascended into glory, he was the firstfruits of that great harvest of men and women from all nations who have been spiritually made alive in Christ (1 Cor. 15:20). Those who have been joined to him can never be separated from his resurrection life. As Jesus

said at the graveside of Lazarus, "I am the resurrection and
the life. Whoever believes in me, though he die, yet shall
he live, and everyone who lives and believes in me shall
never die" (John 11:25–26).

FORGIVING AND BEING FORGIVEN

The central portion of this chapter deals with the interaction between Joseph and his brothers. The reason for this
is that, even though we all need to prepare for death, for
most of us the most pressing issue is how to get through
life. After Jacob's death, all of the old worries resurfaced
in the minds of Joseph's brothers. Had Joseph really forgiven them or had he merely been biding his time to pay
them back for their old crime? So they sent this message
to Joseph:

> Your father gave this command before he died, "Say
> to Joseph, Please forgive the transgression of your
> brothers and their sin, because they did evil to you."
> And now, please forgive the transgression of the
> servants of the God of your father. (Gen. 50:16–17)

It is unlikely that Jacob really said any such thing. If the
message was truly from him, he would surely have spoken
directly to Joseph before he died. Yet the brothers' fears
were groundless. Far from plotting to kill them, Joseph's
response was to weep over their lack of trust (Gen. 50:17).
The reconciliation was real and unfeigned on his part. Their
forgiveness was complete. The brothers had become a
harmonious community of people at last, just as God promised Jacob (35:11). Indeed, Joseph reminded the brothers
that all that had happened was part of God's providence:
they might have intended to harm him, but God intended
it for good, to save the lives of his people (50:20). Why
should he seek to usurp God's place and extract punishment

from them? If God was satisfied, it was not his place to seek revenge. Rather than planning them harm, Joseph would personally (the "I" is emphatic) provide for them and their children (50:21). This is astonishing grace.

There is much for us to reflect on, as those who are both sinners and sinned against. First, Joseph shows us what it means to be forgiven. There is no shallow denial of wrongdoing or pretending that evil has not been done. The brothers didn't blame Jacob's favoritism or Joseph's obnoxiousness for their actions. Nor did Joseph say, "I know that you didn't mean to hurt me. What you did doesn't really matter." On the contrary, the brothers said, "We did evil," and Joseph added, "You meant evil." The brothers actually confessed their sins, and Joseph acknowledged their confession. They all recognized that truly evil things had been done by truly evil men; real people were genuinely hurt. Years were spent in slavery and bondage; hearts were shattered, and lives were torn apart.

What is more, they all acknowledged that that evil deserves to be judged. When Joseph said, "Am I in the place of God?" (Gen. 50:19), he acknowledged that it is God's place to judge evil. The Lord is holy and righteous, and he has declared evil to be under a curse. Joseph chose not to judge them, not because their evil wasn't really so bad, but because there is an ultimate judge who will judge all things righteously. Joseph also reminds us that, even though these things were truly evil and evil truly deserves to be judged, God can also turn evil to good and forgive sinners instead of judging them.

These verses therefore also speak to our need for forgiveness. First, Joseph's words call each of us to face up to the reality of our sin against God and against one another. We don't just make mistakes and accidentally mess up our lives; rather, we sin—boldly, deliberately, and with premeditation. Those who want to spend most of their time talking about what other people have done to them are not yet ready to ask forgiveness. Even amid the experience of suffering significant wrong, we can receive forgiveness only when we truly acknowledge our own sin and recognize that it truly is as evil as has been alleged. Our sin is almost always worse than the allegations against us, because others only see our behavior, while our worst sins are committed in secret in our hearts. We do evil things against others because our hearts are evil, not because our circumstances are difficult and they provoke us to sin.

What is more, that evil deserves to be judged. There is a holy God in heaven who is offended by our sin, even if we manage to avoid all of its earthly consequences. Evil doesn't just evaporate into the atmosphere because we recognize and confess it. If justice and right are to prevail, then evil must be judged. Your sins and mine deserve the punishment of eternal death. However, our God is a redeeming God, who turns evil into good and brings blessing out of things that were intended as curses. Through the death of Joseph's hopes and dreams for a normal life, God brought life and peace for a whole family, protecting them from the famine. What a picture of the gospel that provides for us! By grace, we don't get the judgment that we deserve for our sin. Instead, we get the absolute reverse: God's free, unmerited favor in Jesus Christ. The supreme example of the plans of wicked men being turned around for the good of God's people comes at the cross, as Peter told his hearers on the day of Pentecost:

> This Jesus, delivered up according to the definite plan and foreknowledge of God, you crucified and killed by the hands of lawless men. God raised him up, loosing the pangs of death, because it was not possible for him to be held by it. (Acts 2:23–24)

At the cross, we see both sides of the story. We see evil being judged in the person of Jesus, the only completely innocent person who ever lived. All of God's outrage at the horrific damage that our sin causes in this world was laid upon him. He was cut off from the loving gaze of his Father and enveloped in the coldness and darkness of hell's utter abandonment. But at the cross we also see profound evil being turned around for good, as through that terrible death we are set free from the wrath of God and enveloped in the eternal smile of the Father's favor and blessing. The one who sits in God's place as our judge says to us, "I do not condemn you; now go, and sin no more." What is more, Jesus was buried. Our righteous judge so identified with us in death that his bones lay in a tomb for three days. Jesus staked his eternity on the Father's power to break death's grip on him and raise him up as the firstfruits of the resurrection.

GRASPING THE FATHER'S FORGIVENESS

Just as the brothers had a hard time believing Joseph had really forgiven them, so too you and I struggle to grasp the fullness of the Father's forgiveness. Joseph had done everything possible to demonstrate the completeness of his forgiveness, yet his brothers still did not trust him. They were convinced that he was just waiting to judge them. So too, many of us struggle to appropriate the forgiveness we have received. We live our lives fearful of God's impending judgment, interpreting every negative circumstance as evidence that God is out to get us. If a loved one dies, or a precious relationship ends, or you don't get the promotion you desire, or even if the car won't start, you doubt whether God really loves you. You are sure that this is evidence that he has planned ruin for your life. Yet how much more clearly can he show you his forgiveness? God crucified his only Son for you; how will he not also, along with him, give you everything you need for life and godliness? Think how hard it must have been for the Father to close his ears to the desperate cries of his beloved, only begotten Son! If he bore that pain for you then, will he give you up now? If you are a believer in Christ today, your sins really are forgiven, nailed to the cross with Christ, and buried in the ocean depths of his love for you. His provision for you in Christ is sure and certain and cannot be broken by your ongoing sin and failure.

This passage also addresses us as those who are sinned against, and calls us in our dealings with one another to live out of the reality of the forgiveness we have received. We must learn to forgive as we have been forgiven—not to return evil for evil, but instead to return good (Rom. 12:21). Paul reminds us that we cannot repair every broken relationship; it is not always in our power to make others live at peace with us (12:18). However, it is always open to us to seek to return good for evil, to feed our hungry enemies, and to give a cup of cold water to them when they are thirsty (12:20). It is possible for us to show extraordinary, gospel-driven kindness to people who have utterly forfeited any claim to our affections through the evil they have done to us, whether they recognize it and repent of it or not.

That is incredibly hard to do. Our hearts cry out, "Somebody needs to pay for what they have done." That is true: somebody must pay for what they have done. In Romans 12:19, Paul goes on to say (quoting Deuteronomy 32:35), "Vengeance is mine, I will repay, says the Lord." There is a judge who will see that every evil receives its due penalty. But since you and I are not that judge, we don't need to extract payment for evil. Instead, we are set free to forgive, releasing that evil and freeing ourselves from its stranglehold over our hearts. Instead of being overcome by the power of evil, good once again overcomes evil as the Holy Spirit enables us to forgive and show kindness even to those who don't deserve it. The cross bears rich fruit in our lives, so that we start to forgive as we have been forgiven.

THE FRUIT OF THE CROSS

The richest fruit of the cross, though, is not in our forgiving others, but in the forgiveness that we ourselves have received. While we remain here on earth, we will continue to struggle to forgive others and to believe that we ourselves are truly forgiven. Our experience here on earth is one of constant waiting and longing, living by faith in the gap between what God has promised and the reality that confronts our eyes. That is why the last words of the book of Genesis are not words about Joseph's forgiveness, but words about Joseph's dying faith in a deliverance that was yet to come. The book of Genesis began with a man in a garden, enjoying God's presence; it ends with a man in a coffin, looking forward to a restoration of that presence. The bitter effects of sin are dreadfully clear: death has invaded the world through sin and holds us all captive to its power. Yet the faith of the man whose remains are in that coffin speaks equally loudly of God's purpose to break sin's power and save a people through his sovereign choice of Abraham and his descendants to become God's redeemed people.

Those descendants of Abraham didn't merit God's choice any more than he did: it is all of grace, from beginning to end. But through faith, Abraham, Isaac, Jacob, and all of his offspring looked forward to receiving the promise, a promise that we also have received along with them. Here on earth, the years of our pilgrimage may be "few and difficult," like Jacob's early years in Paddan-aram and Canaan, or full of blessing, like his last years in Egypt. Whatever our experience in this world, if we are trusting in Christ, then we may have the same assurance that the Lord will be our God and that his presence will abide with us. As a result, we can live without fear, confident that God loves us and watches over us for Christ's sake.

What is more, when the time comes for us to die, we too can lay down our bones in the solid hope of the resurrection of the dead. We may mourn and be devastated by the death of those whom we love. Death is still an enemy to us all. Yet he is now a defeated enemy, whose sting has been drawn by the death and resurrection of Jesus, the firstfruits of our full inheritance. As the founder and perfecter of our faith (Heb. 12:2), he gives us the perfect righteousness we need to stand before God without fear. As surely as Jesus Christ is risen, so surely may we look forward to eternity with him. Death is not the end; it is not merely riding off into the sunset. It is riding off into the sunrise, a sunrise illuminated by the light that beams from the face of our risen Lord. As John Donne put it so beautifully:

> One short sleep past, we wake eternally,
> And death shall be no more; Death, thou shalt die.

FOR FURTHER REFLECTION

1. How did the deaths of Jacob and Joseph highlight their faith and point forward to God's future salvation?
2. What are some different ideas about what it means to die well?
3. What has been the focus of funeral services you've attended? Have the funerals of Christians been different from the funerals of non-Christians?
4. Joseph reiterated his forgiveness of his brothers. What does true forgiveness (extended and received) look like? How does it deal with past sins, evil committed, and guilt? What does the cross teach us about forgiveness?
5. How has the overall story of Joseph and his family helped you understand forgiveness and reconciliation? How has the story of this family helped you understand the relevance of Jesus' life, death, and resurrection in your life?

NOTES

CHAPTER ONE: HOPE FOR DYSFUNCTIONAL FAMILIES

1 In the Pentateuch, the Septuagint normally translates *qahal* by *synagoge*, but the basic point is still valid.

2 Victor P. Hamilton, *The Book of Genesis 18–50* (Grand Rapids: Eerdmans, 1995), 406.

CHAPTER TWO: SHATTERED DREAMS

1 *Les Misérables*: lyrics by Herbert Kretzmer; music by Alain Boublil and Claude-Michel Schönberg; based on the novel by Victor Hugo.

2 Sidney Greidanus, *Preaching Christ from Genesis* (Grand Rapids: Eerdmans, 2007), 338.

CHAPTER THREE: A BREAKTHROUGH FOR VICTIMS AND SINNERS

1 Gordon J. Wenham, *Genesis 16–50* (Dallas: Word Books, 1994), 366.

2 Sidney Greidanus, *Preaching Christ from Genesis* (Grand Rapids: Eerdmans, 2007), 369 n. 29.

3 Miroslav Volf, *Exclusion and Embrace: A Theological Exploration of Identity, Otherness and Reconciliation* (Nashville: Abingdon, 1996), 80–81.

4 Ibid.

CHAPTER FOUR: GOD'S WONDERFUL PLAN

1 See Paul David Tripp, *Instruments in the Redeemer's Hands: People in Need of Change Helping People in Need of Change* (Phillipsburg, NJ: P&R, 2002), 77–78.

2 Claus Westermann, *Genesis 37–50* (Minneapolis: Fortress, 2002), 67.

CHAPTER FIVE: WHEN HOPE GETS PUT ON HOLD

1 Bruce K. Waltke with Cathi J. Fredericks, *Genesis: A Commentary* (Grand Rapids: Zondervan, 2001), 526.

CHAPTER SEVEN: REUNION OR RECONCILIATION?

1 "Paradise by the Dashboard Light," words and music by Jim Steinman, © CBS 1977.

CHAPTER TEN: FROM FAMINE TO FORTUNE

1 The blanks in their conversation are highlighted by Bruce K. Waltke with Cathi J. Fredericks, *Genesis: A Commentary* (Grand Rapids: Zondervan, 2001), 569–70.

2 "The Passing of the Elves," *The Fellowship of the Ring*, extended edition, directed by Peter Jackson (2001; New Line Home Video, 2002), DVD.

CHAPTER ELEVEN: BETTER THAN WE DESERVE

1 Bruce K. Waltke with Cathi J. Fredericks, *Genesis: A Commentary* (Grand Rapids: Zondervan, 2001), 591.

CHAPTER TWELVE: FAMOUS LAST WORDS

1 Christopher Hitchens, "Trial of the Will," *Vanity Fair*, January 2012. http://www.vanityfair.com/culture/2012/01/hitchens-201201 (accessed February 15, 2012).

CHAPTER THIRTEEN: MIXED BLESSINGS

1 Bruce K. Waltke with Cathi J. Fredericks, *Genesis: A Commentary* (Grand Rapids: Zondervan, 2001), 613.

CHAPTER FOURTEEN: DEAD AND BURIED?

1 John Donne, "Holy Sonnets, 10," in *The Complete English Poems* (London: Penguin, 1977), 313.

INDEX OF SCRIPTURE

ALSO BY IAIN M. DUGUID

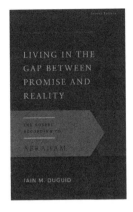 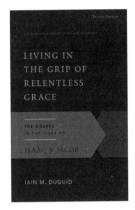

Living in the Gap between Promise and Reality: The Gospel According to Abraham

"Jesus explained that all the Scriptures that had preceeded him were about him. This means that if we preach of teach on any passage of the Old Testament and do not speak of him, we fail to mention the very thing that Jesus said the passage is about. . . . I am grateful for this eminently accessible book. . . . which closes the gap between Christ's redemptive work and the life of Abraham."

—Bryan Chapell

Living in the Grip of Relentless Grace: The Gospel According to Isaac and Jacob

"Iain Duguid is both a first-class scholar and a gifted preacher. This book is theologically astute, Christ centered, and extremely practical. A tremendous resource."

—Timothy J. Keller

ALSO BY IAIN M. DUGUID

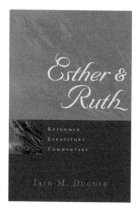 

Esther & Ruth

"Iain Duguid brings it all together: a specialist's knowledge of the Hebrew text and culture, a preacher's eye for theme and structure, a pastor's skill in nuanced application, a theologian's grasp of Christ-centered theology (that would make Geerhardus Vos smile), and a wordsmith's attention to language and lingering metaphor."

—R. Kent Hughes

Song of Songs

"Here's the work of a multigifted scholar on display! Here Iain Duguid is the expositor, the biblical theologian, the pastor, the counselor, and—quite often!—the surgeon. This exposition is vintage Duguid—sneakingly convicting and awash in grace. He lures me to oversimplify: if someone asks me how best to prepare for marriage, I will be tempted to say, 'Study the Song of Songs and read Duguid's commentary.'"

—Dale Ralph Davis

ALSO IN THE REFORMED EXPOSITORY COMMENTARY SERIES

 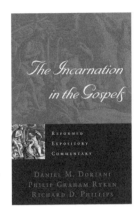

Each volume in the Reformed Expository Commentary series provides exposition that gives careful attention to the biblical text, is doctrinally Reformed, focuses on Christ through the lens of redemptive history, and applies the Bible to our contemporary setting.

ALSO BY IAIN M. DUGUID

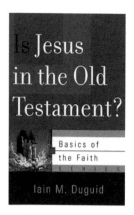

Many Christians find the Old Testament to be a difficult book and ultimately ignore large parts of it—often because they simply are not sure what to do with it.

Yet Iain Duguid maintains that the Old Testament is for Christians too. What is more, Christ is present throughout the Old Testament—in fact, when rightly interpreted, the whole book is about him. Duguid explores what it means to rightly see Christ in the Old Testament and looks at some specific ways the Old Testament prepares us to see and understand Christ's ministry in the gospels.

MORE TITLES IN THE BASICS
OF THE FAITH SERIES

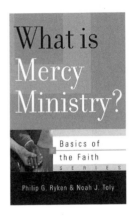

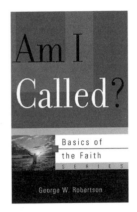

Basics of the Faith booklets introduce readers to basic Reformed doctrine and practice. On issues of church government and practice they reflect that framework—otherwise they are suitable for all church situations.

What is a True Calvinist?, Philip Graham Ryken

What is a Reformed Church?, Stephen Smallman

What is True Conversion?, Stephen Smallman

What is the Lord's Supper?, Richard D. Philips

What is the Christian Worldview?, Philip Graham Ryken

What Are Election and Predestination?, Richard D. Philips

How Our Children Come to Faith, Stephen Smallman

Why Do We Baptize Infants?, Bryan Chapell

What Is Justification by Faith Alone?, J. V. Fesko

How Do We Glorify God?, John D. Hannah

Barbara Duguid turns to the writings of John Newton to teach us God's purpose for our failure and guilt—and to help us adjust our expectations of ourselves. Her empathetic, honest approach lifts our focus from our own performance back to the God who is bigger than our failures—and who uses them for his glory. Rediscover how God's extravagant grace makes the gospel once again feel like the good news it truly is!

"Take this book to heart. It will sustain you for the long haul, long after the hyped-up panaceas and utopias fail."
   —David Powlison

"Barb tells the story of God's unrelenting compassion toward sinners like us with profound wisdom."
   —Michael S. Horton

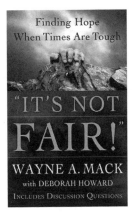

When people complain about their lot in life, thinking God is not treating them as he should, they need to read *It's Not Fair!* This book comes alongside people right where they are and moves them to a place where they can finally rest in God's attributes of omniscience, omnipotence, love, and justice through the use of sound biblical encouragement.

"A simple yet profound and practical book. Since we are all prone to murmur against God's kind providence, everyone should read this book."
　—Joel R. Beeke

"An honest assessment of how we have allowed contemporary notions of fairness to rule our hearts rather than coming to grips with the true nature of God and His character."
　—Lance Quinn

ALSO FROM P&R PUBLISHING

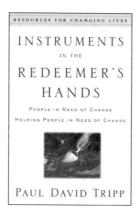

We might be relieved if God placed our sanctification only in the hands of trained professionals, but that is not his plan. Instead, through the ministry of every part of the body, the whole church will mature in Christ.

Paul David Tripp helps us discover where change is needed in our own lives and the lives of others. Following the example of Jesus, Tripp reveals how to get to know people and how to lovingly speak truth to them.

"A wonderful application of the old Gaelic saying, 'God strikes straight blows with crooked sticks.' As inadequate as we are, God is eager to use us to help others change. The more you apply the biblical principles discussed in this book, the more readily you will fit into his mighty hand."
—**Ken Sande**